Praise for

Transitioning Clients and the Retirement Exit Decision

by Christine Timms

"Christine Timms, a seasoned financial advisor with a 30 year track record in the business, has shared in a succinct and timely way, all the secrets you need to know to successfully make your retirement transition. With checklists, templates, and carefully articulated steps, Christine provides the roadmap for sustaining a successful transition. Advisors would be wise to study this handbook and consider it their primary source of advice."

—Susan Latremoille
Former Financial Advisor
35 year veteran of the financial advisory business
Author of *The RichLife - Managing Wealth and Purpose*
Coauthor of *Thriving Throughout Your Retirement Transition*
Founder of Next Chapter Lifestyle Advisors

"My associate and I have found *Transitioning Clients and the Retirement Exit Decision* to be very helpful. Although we had done our own work prior in this area, the questions (steps of transition, choose your successor, contract, process of informing clients, final thoughts) acted as a "playbook" that we are further integrating. To us, it is providing more confidence we are addressing all areas and checking off everything. Having this organization will ensure nothing falls through the cracks. Your model provides additional confidence for a transition that will be successful for clients and ultimately all stakeholders."

—Kevin Punshon
Financial Advisor for over 30 years
Chairman's Club member
Branch Manager
Big Five Canadian Bank owned brokerage firm

CT Financial™

Handbooks for the Professional Financial Advisor

Transitioning Clients

and the

Retirement Exit Decision

Includes Strategies and Tools for Seeking and Implementing Group Referrals

Christine Timms

Paperback ISBN: 978-1-7773145-4-5
French Flap Paperback ISBN: 978-1-7773145-5-2
ePub ISBN: 978-1-7773145-6-9
MOBI ISBN: 978-1-7773145-7-6
PDF ISBN: 978-1-7773453-6-5
Audiobook ISBN: 978-1-7773453-3-4

Published by CT Financial Press

Cover design by CT Financial Press & Melissa Levesque

Edited by Kristen Silva

Refer to www.ChristineTimms.com to buy handbooks and templates from the "Handbooks for the Professional Financial Advisor" series

Care has been taken to trace ownership of copyright material contained in this text. The publisher will gladly receive any information that will enable any reference or credit line to be rectified in subsequent editions.

Important Disclaimer: This publication is sold with the understanding that (I) the author is not responsible for the results of any actions taken on the basis of information in this work, nor for any errors or omissions; and (2) the author is not engaged in rendering investment, financial planning, legal, accounting or other professional services. The author expressly disclaims all and any liability to any person, whether a purchaser of this publication or not, in respect of anything and of the consequences of anything done or omitted to be done by any such person in reliance, whether whole or partial, upon the whole or any part of the contents of this publication. If legal advice or other expert assistance is required, the services of a competent professional person should be sought.

I dedicate this book to
Adrian Bannister, the love of my life, and
Peter Bannister, the best son a mother could wish for.

Contents

Introduction to the Handbooks for the Professional Financial Advisor Series

I see myself as a client advocate who believes the best way to help financial services clients is to help the advisors who give independent financial advice. For the purposes of this series, I will define a financial advisor as an individual looking to provide services relating to investments, financial planning and/or insurance to individuals and small businesses. I believe that clients are best served by continuous long-term relationships with human advisors who seek to understand and work with the client to achieve the client's goals. The following quote from a note I received from a couple upon my retirement confirms that belief:

> "In wishing you the best, we want to thank you and your team for looking after our investments so well over the last 20 years. With a high level of professionalism, you have guided us through good times and bad with the consistent proven good advice to 'stay the course'. Throughout, you have communicated openly, proactively and reviewed and reported on our circumstances consistently. Not only did you provide guidance with our investment portfolio but also took the time to advise us in the overlapping areas of tax issues, insurance benefits, estate planning and will preparation. Lastly our yearly reviews were not only extremely helpful but cemented the personal relationships. Thank you!"
>
> —retired couple

I believe that by helping advisors succeed, I will help financial services clients succeed. I am also hoping that management of advisor firms, regulators and industry product/service suppliers will read these handbooks to gain a deeper awareness of the uniqueness and needs of both advisors and advisors' clients.

A financial advisor's job has always been stressful due to the unpredictability of financial markets and the people issues of any service industry. I believe the job is even more difficult today because of increased competition, the expansion of potential services (financial planning, etc.) and the growing number of investments available as well as increasing regulatory requirements. The good news is that advisors who use constantly evolving fintech and processes to improve their services and efficiency are able to increase the capacity and profitability of their practice while making advice available to more people.

I have written these handbooks to coach and assist advisors hoping to help reduce their stress and increase their productivity. I present ideas and processes relating to all aspects of a financial services practice with an emphasis on services, organization and preparedness. Preparedness reduces the stress of encounters with clients, prospects, markets, etc. Having a clearly articulated business plan, sharing the workload with a team and having a succession plan in place all work to reduce the stress of the business while making it easier to serve more clients effectively and profitably. The ideas are intended to help all advisors regardless of their unique approach to investing and client service, their unique clientele and their practice size. I hope to make it easier for advisors to serve their clients well, to the benefit of all stakeholders in a strong, sustainable financial advice industry (clients, advisors, advisors' firms, product providers).

As you might expect, this means sharing my experiences from my 33-year career as a financial advisor and showing what I learned from my mistakes. However, it also means sharing many templates and calculators (downloadable from my website) to help advisors easily implement the ideas that I share. During my career, I attended many practice management seminars agreeing with much of the advice given, but failing to implement the ideas because it would take too much time to do so. I am going to provide templates and calculators using my practice as an example, but I fully expect advisors to edit, modify and customize them to match their personal approach and the needs of their unique clientele. My customizable templates will help an advisor implement the ideas quickly as it is much easier to edit, modify and customize than it is to create from scratch.

> *"I really like your approach and, in particular, all the useful templates and checklists you provide. It is far more practical than many practice management books I have read over the 32 years I have been in the industry."*
>
> —Gary Mayzes
> Senior management of a Big Five Canadian Bank

I have been asked if these handbooks are intended to be "best practices for financial advisors." I hope they are "good practices for financial advisors" handbooks. I can't possibly claim "best" practices as I know there are many techniques and processes created by many advisors and/or firms that I am not even aware of.

I enjoyed helping many advisors over the years, sometimes formally under a firm inspired mentor program and sometimes through seminars sanctioned by management. However, most of my mentoring was "ad hoc" primarily for advisors within my own firm whom I met at conferences or within my own branch. These books are an opportunity to provide more complete and thorough mentoring for more financial advisors with practices in all financial services channels ranging from the large bank dealer to the financial planner operating as a sole practitioner.

> "I have been in the business for 25+ years working in various management roles. I have worked with many investment advisors in my career and must tell you from a 'client first mindset', Chris is one of the best. ... We could all learn a thing or two from Chris."
>
> —Wilma Ditchfield
> Senior management of a Big Five Canadian Bank

Handbooks in the Series

As I write this introduction to my series of handbooks for financial advisors, I have essentially completed handbooks regarding business models, team building, and transitioning clients and the retirement exit decision. I expect to complete another handbook about presentations and processes in the near future.

These books will reflect my strong belief that the "win-win" approach builds happier, sustainable relationships with all the stakeholders of your practice (clients, team members, branch management, service/product providers and senior firm management). The win-win concept does not mean that you compromise your own benefits but rather you grow the size of the pie to be shared so that all parties receive more—it is winning alongside each of the other stakeholders of your practice.

I recommend reading the entire series of handbooks once even though some areas may not seem immediately applicable to your practice. For example, you may think you are too young to consider the chapters relating to retirement or transitioning a clientele; however, you are likely not too young to think about pursuing a group referral of clients from another advisor. An advisor approaching retirement may initially see no need to read the business models handbook; however, upon reading it, they will see how they can easily articulate and compare their business model to that of the appropriate successor advisor. I have provided a detailed table of contents in each book to provide a quick overview and to help you easily refer to specific topics as the need arises over time.

Business Models for Financial Advisors

"You have set a great example for others running a very strong and successful practice.... I always knew your clients were very well taken care of."

—Steve Geist
Former Group Head - Wealth Management
Canadian Imperial Bank of Commerce

A well-articulated, written business model is a valuable tool for advisors at all stages of their career. An Advisor's deeper understanding of their own practice and who it serves best, will lead to sustainable relationships based on a win-win business model. I will define an advisor's business model as the articulation of who the advisor's most compatible clients are, the services and products that the advisor offers those clients, how those products/services are provided, how clients are charged and how the advisor is paid. I show how advisors in all stages of their careers can benefit from a well-defined business model, even those about to retire. The handbook provides a checklist process to quickly articulate, develop or analyze an existing or desired unique business model. I provide an example of the process by showing completed checklists based on the final years of my practice and the resulting printed business model. I include discussions regarding many of the required decisions as we progress through the checklists for the various business model components. I also discuss household capacity of practices and provide an analytical tool and checklists to facilitate the segmentation of clientele. This handbook includes appendices "Why Advisors are Not Interchangeable", "Why Many Full-Service Independent Revenue Sharing Advisors Have and Deserve Above Average Incomes" and "The Average Advisor of Various Financial Advice Channels."

Team Building for Financial Advisors

> *"Chris always seemed to gather people around that seemed to know what they were doing, they were young and learning the business, but they always struck me as being competent. But more than that, they seem to recognize the interests of the client, and they look after the client just as well as Chris does. In other words, they reflected her."*

—Dennis Dack (client of 30 years)
Retired Director of Strategic Policy
Advisor to the Chairman of the Board
Ontario Hydro

My team played a huge part in my overall success. I believe that my business would have plateaued at about 20% of my final practice (assets under management and revenue) if I had not built a team. This handbook focuses on the benefits of team building, delegating, supervising, outsourcing, hiring, training, team structure, compensation, motivation, turnover, etc. Team building is another classic example of a win-win approach to business. All of the stakeholders in an advisor's practice (clients, team members, advisor and firm) win from the advisor's ability to work with and delegate to team members. My willingness to build and nurture a team allowed me to expand my service to existing clients and pursue more clients resulting in a bigger and happier clientele, which naturally produced more revenue to be shared by myself, my team members and my firm.

Transitioning Clients and the Retirement Exit Decision

> *"Chris cared and continues to care about her clients - absolutely evident in her approach to her team and her solid plan for her retirement and the transition of her clients to the RIGHT advisors. The final proof is her two successors' very high client retention rate three years after her retirement."*
>
> —Wilma Ditchfield
> Senior management of a Big Five Canadian Bank

I retired with the largest assets under management and highest annual revenue of my career. I believe this was partially due to high client retention in my later years as clients were aware of my succession plans years before I actually announced my retirement. Three years after my retirement the assets and revenue generated from the clients transitioned to my successors were higher than when I left.

The handbook contains three interrelated topics:

1) Seeking Group Referrals from Another Advisor
2) Transitioning Your Clientele to Your Successor
3) The Retirement Exit Decision

The need to transition clients from one advisor to another advisor can be triggered by many different circumstances. An advisor will make group referrals to a successor advisor when they are retiring, reducing their clientele or changing their business model. The key to a successful transition of clients is compatibility between the successor, referring advisor and the clientele being referred. I believe this compatibility is more likely to be achieved when the successor and the referring advisor understand each other's positions and business models. Reading all three topics will provide the reader with needed insight and understanding in addition to providing step-by-step processes and tools to complete the transition.

Deciding when to retire is a very personal decision. I give my own reasons in "Why I Retired" as well as what I enjoy most about being retired. In "Hints That It May Be Time to Start Preparing for Retirement", I have provided a list of possible reasons for retiring that I have experienced or learned from others in the financial advice industry. I then point out many of the personal and business dangers of waiting too long to retire. Finally, I outline several steps that I recommend in preparation for an advisor's retirement.

Future Handbook on Processes and Presentations

I have gathered much of the content but have yet to complete the handbook relating to processes and presentations. This book will provide a lot of the "nuts and bolts" needed to implement an advisor's business model. Our presentations and interactions with clients showed them that we understood them and their needs making it easier for clients to trust us and understand our advice. The use of systematic processes and templates by yourself and your team will enable efficient delegation and supervision of the performance of many of the activities needed to find and service your sustainable client base and help you run your practice. During my career, my team and I developed many detailed presentations and processes including templates, calculators and macros for all six of the business model components with an emphasis on the major categories of the service model. These processes along with a good contact management system (client relationship management software or CRM) allowed me to grow my clientele and expand both my team and services. This handbook will discuss processes and presentations in great detail for each business model component and provide tools and templates to help advisors easily implement and customize the ideas that appeal to them.

I hope these handbooks leave advisors with a lot to think about, some ideas relevant to their practice and the means to implement those ideas.

> *"I have found all three of these books to be very thought provoking, not only as it relates to the information provided, but also from looking forward within the context of my own practice and my own personal plan for the next stage of my life."*
> —Rollie Guenette
> Financial Advisor for over 25 years
> Chairman's Club member
> Big Five Canadian bank owned brokerage firm

Transitioning Clients
and the
Retirement Exit Decision

Introduction

The handbook contains three interrelated topics:

Part 1. Seeking Group Referrals from Another Advisor

Part 2. Transitioning Your Clientele to Your Successor

Part 3. The Retirement Exit Decision

The need to transition clients from one advisor to another advisor can be triggered by many different circumstances. An advisor will make group referrals to a successor advisor when they are retiring, reducing their clientele or changing their business model. The key to a successful transition of clients is compatibility between the successor, referring advisor and the clientele being referred. I believe this compatibility is more likely to be achieved when the successor and the referring advisor understand each other's situation. Reading all three topics and the tools provided by the handbook and my website should facilitate this understanding.

The first part "Seeking Group Referrals from Another Advisor" is intended to focus on the successor or potential successor's point of view. The "Transitioning Your Clientele to Your Successor" part will focus primarily on the perspective of the advisor who is referring the clientele. Many issues overlap, and I have chosen to include more details of the overlapping issues in "Transitioning Your Clientele to Your Successor" to minimize repetition. I believe both the successor and the referring advisor benefit greatly by understanding each other's position and business model. Reading both parts as well as "The Retirement Exit Decision" should be beneficial to all concerned. Going forward in this book, I will often identify the advisor who is referring the clientele as the "retiree." The reference to a retiree will sometimes include advisors who are transitioning a portion of their clientele to a new advisor without retiring.

Deciding when to retire is a very personal decision. I give my own reasons in "Why I Retired" as well as what I enjoy most about being retired. In "Hints That It May Be Time to Start Preparing for Retirement", I have provided a list of possible reasons for retiring that I have experienced or learned from others in the financial advice industry. I then point out many of the personal and business dangers of waiting too long to retire. Finally, I outline several steps that I recommend in preparation for an advisor's retirement.

This handbook also includes an appendix to help advisors seeking group referrals and retiring advisors determine their compatibility with each other through the articulation of their business models.

PART ONE: Seeking Group Referrals from Another Advisor

Assuming another advisor's clientele can be an excellent opportunity to build your practice. However, you need to be aware of the additional time, work and financial commitments you will be undertaking. A successful integration of the new clients into your practice should have no impact on your pre-existing clients. You need to be willing to sacrifice your time and aspects of your personal life during the transition period (probably for at least a year).

In this part of the book, I will discuss the following:

- positioning yourself to be chosen as a successor
- client referral opportunities
- my experience assuming part of a retiring advisor's clientele
- preparing to integrate another advisor's clients into your own practice

Positioning Yourself to be Chosen as a Successor

Advisors generally choose successors that they know, like and trust. If you would like to be thought of as a potential successor to another advisor's practice/clientele, consider doing the following:

1) Mingle and get to know other advisors at firm gatherings, branch meetings, parties, etc.

2) Be willing to share and discuss business ideas with other advisors.

3) Maintain a good reputation for treating your clients, your team and fellow advisors well.

4) Maintain a good relationship with your branch manager.

5) Develop and maintain a good relationship with higher levels of management when possible.

6) Work to understand and empathize with the issues and feelings of an advisor who is contemplating retirement. Reading parts two and three of this book, "Transitioning Your Clientele to Your Successor" and "The Retirement Exit Decision" should help you put yourself in the shoes of an advisor who is contemplating retirement.

7) Work to understand and empathize with advisors who are considering significant changes to their practice, such as investment strategy, fee structure, service model, etc. They may consider referring a portion of their clientele to you if some of their clients are not compatible with the changes they plan on making to their practice.

8) Be prepared to provide a potential referring advisor with a document describing your unique business model in detail. This description of your business model will help the referring advisor assess your compatibility with their clientele and your compatibility with what the advisor thinks the clientele will need in the future. To enable advisors to create their own business model document with minimal cost and effort, my website offers an Excel spreadsheet checklist process to help advisors quickly identify most, if not all, aspects of their business model. I have provided all of the checklists in the form of a fully completed sample including the resulting summary in the Appendix of this book. A fully articulated business model should include a description of your existing clientele and the services you provide to those clients including the methods of client contact, your approach to investing and financial planning as well as how clients are charged. The checklists and related macros will also facilitate a quick comparison to another advisor's business model making it easier to identify similarities and

differences. The referring advisor who also completes the checklists will be able to compare their business model to potential successors. The successor will be able to use the comparison to prepare a plan for integrating new clients into their practice. My handbook *Business Models for Financial Advisors* discusses all aspects of various business models in more detail.

Attention to all of the above items, especially the articulation of your unique business model, should build the confidence of the referring advisor and the firm's management. It will show your professionalism and potential ability to successfully transition the referred clients, therefore increasing your chances of being chosen as a successor.

Clientele Referral Opportunities

Opportunities for group referrals will arise when an advisor is retiring or reducing their clientele. An advisor will consider reducing their clientele when they change their approach to investing, change their approach to fees or commissions, achieve work-life balance or for many other personal/business reasons. For example, an older advisor may wish to reduce travel to out of office appointments. I have also seen a case where a retiring independent financial planner chose a successor in a different advice channel (a full-service bank owned brokerage firm) to handle clients' investments while continuing to provide tax return preparation services.

About 20 years into my career as a financial advisor, I fully committed to managed money for the common equity portion of clients' portfolios and stopped picking individual stocks. I then referred a group of clients who still wanted stock picking services to another advisor in my branch. Over ten years later, the successor advisor is still happy with the transition and has informed me that she still receives quality referrals from the families of the original group referral.

Advisors looking for successors may or may not be able to find a successor advisor who is easily identified as compatible.

Potential Levels of Compatibility

I think most transitions will fall into one or a combination of the four different scenarios below, listed in the order of the highest likely client retention:

1) You are extremely involved in the service of the retiree's clients before assuming the clientele. You are the retiree's associate or partner and therefore have a very compatible investment strategy and service model.

2) You are not involved with the retiree's clients but have an investment strategy and service model compatible with the referring advisor's clientele's future needs.

3) You are taking over from a retiring advisor who believes their existing investment strategy and/or service model needs to be modified. The advisor may see the need to be more managed money, globally diversified, and/or fee-based but is not willing to do the required work at this stage of their career.

4) You are not involved and have a significantly different investment style.

- My retirement was a scenario 1 transition. Associates from my team were my successors.

- My group referral of clients, when I stopped picking common stocks, was a combination of scenario 2 and 3 transitions.

- The partial clientele that I assumed was a scenario 4 transition. I was not involved with any of the retiring advisor's clients and, as I discovered after taking over the clientele, we had a significantly different investment style.

My Experience Assuming Part of a Retiring Advisor's Clientele

In August 1998, 18 years before I retired, an advisor in my branch became ill; after a few months, he determined that he could not return to work for health reasons. I knew he had health issues and made it known to my manager that I was willing to consider compensating the retiring advisor for the referral of all or part of his clientele. We were not friends outside the office but had worked together on a prospecting project briefly and had attended some meetings together regarding real estate limited partnerships. We discussed the industry and our businesses during car rides to the limited partnership meetings. We had also shared an assistant for a year or two. We were both Chairman's Club members and had similar revenue and assets. We were both cold callers, hard-working and ambitious. He chose me to assume a little less than half of his clientele and his associate assumed the rest. My manager recently told me that the advisor chose me because he respected me and liked the way I managed my practice. I think he liked my work ethic and knew that I cared about my clients.

When I agreed to assume the part of the practice offered to me, my firm decided on the referral compensation and transition payment schedule. I went along without really knowing if it was a good deal or not. I believed the retiring advisor had a good number of high net worth clients because he had recommended limited partnerships to many of his clients, and those partnerships were only appropriate for top income earners. I believed it was a rare opportunity that I should not pass up, even though I was busy with my own clients and getting married three months later. I knew it was a gamble, but I also knew my expenses, including the transition payments, were covered by my pre-existing practice. I stopped all prospecting and focused on the inherited clients while maintaining service to my existing clients. Because of his illness, we had no discussions regarding his investment strategy and no joint meetings with his clients. He simply called his clients and told them I would be calling. Unfortunately, his health was such that he was advised not to do more.

I remember that the clients' portfolios contained a lot of limited partnerships and Canadian resource stocks. There were a few bonds, very few foreign stocks and very few, if any, mutual funds. Although I was familiar with the particular limited partnerships, our approach to investing was very different.

I arranged face-to-face meetings with every client as soon as possible. During the meetings, I presented my "peace of mind" approach to investing to help determine the level of risk appropriate for them. Clients liked the simplicity of my use of a government bond ladder for the safer portion of their investments and saw the benefits of our well diversified stock portfolios and global diversification. I was recommending a mix of equity mutual funds with geographic exposure of 30% Canadian and 70% US/International. I was not yet familiar enough with separately managed accounts to be recommending them. At the time, I was still recommending an individual stock portfolio of 30% Canadian/70% US stocks and international ADRs to all my clients who were not comfortable with mutual funds.

As you might expect, we lost a number of his clients. However, many of the clients who stayed gave us significantly more to invest, often all their investable assets. We maintained the $77 million asset total (excluding future referrals from those clients) for a full year and still maintained 92% of the assets four years later (October 2002). The stock markets were not a factor as they were slightly lower at the end of the four years.

I paid for the referral of his clientele with 36 equal monthly payments. Within 14 months, I had earned enough from the practice to pay for it. In my final year (over 16 years after the transition began), I was still earning over 60% of the cost of the practice. We had fewer clients, but the remaining clients' average household total investments under our care was three times the average household size compared to the beginning of the transition.

It is clearly more difficult to transition a practice under scenario 4 where you were not previously involved with the retiree's clients and have a significantly different investment style. Scenario 4 transitions are a big gamble for the successor, and you should expect to lose some clients. However, you should also expect to receive more business from the clients you keep. The risk of a scenario 4 transition will usually justify significantly lower referral compensation.

The transition worked out very well for me. I believe my success was due to the following:

1) I was at a stage in my life where I was able to work long hours during the week and on weekends without harming my health or my personal life. My husband was also hard-working, and we had no children yet.

2) My team was large (five assistants), well trained and hard-working.

3) I was committed to an investment strategy and approach to risk assessment that new clients easily understood.

4) My unique "current" spreadsheet summarized client holdings concisely, allowing both myself and the client to understand their investment portfolio very quickly in the context of my "peace of mind" approach to investing and assessing risk.

5) I had no financial stress because I knew that the revenue from my existing practice could cover all of my personal and business expenses.

6) I was also lucky, as I had done very little to determine if the price was right.

My manager believes my success came from meeting each client immediately and showing conviction in my investment strategy.

Preparing to Integrate Another Advisor's Clients into Your Own Practice

The process of integrating a large group of clients into your practice is extremely demanding and time intensive. You need individual face-to-face meetings with each client as soon as possible. Your meeting preparation, processes and efficiency are extremely important so that you can maximize your productivity in the time you have available.

Assuming the partial clientele triggered a need for me to improve my processes and develop a written meeting agenda — a precursor to those I intend to show in my advisor's handbook about presentations and processes. We were seeing two to four new clients a day. Although I had a routine, there was no printed appointment booklet, and I did not have a printed agenda. I had a collection of loose papers, including an earlier version of my current investments report containing the client's portfolio. I used a short seminar to explain my approach to investing and we discussed fees/costs. There was nothing that provided the clients with notes from the meeting. Next, I took them through an earlier version of my investment allocation decision process. I promised to prepare recommendations corresponding to the allocations that the client and I determined they would be comfortable with. As you will see in my future processes and presentations handbook, my team and I have greatly improved our processes and templates since then.

If you have your own templates for meetings and other reports, you will be able to delegate much of the appointment preparation to your team. You will be well prepared and therefore more relaxed and confident in the meetings with your new clients. You would be wise to include an associate/assistant in all client meetings for note taking, relationship building, etc. My handbook on team building goes into much more detail regarding how to make the best use of your team.

You and your team should expect to work longer hours as you spend the time required to establish new relationships with clients from the referring advisor. It is important to ensure that service to your previously existing clients does not suffer. You should consider adding a new team member possibly from the referring advisor's team. You should also make sure the compensation of your team members reflects their effort and responsibilities in the integrated practice.

Make sure your website is up to date and shows everything that you would want your new clients to see. If you are going to need new or modified office space, start the process early. If you are going to need to run discretionary accounts, work on your Portfolio Manager designation immediately; it may take longer than you think even if you think you have all the required courses.

Assuming a practice is not a gift, but rather an opportunity that requires a substantial time and financial commitment from you, the successor. Make sure you will still be able to cover your business and living expenses under worse case scenarios. I know an advisor who was an associate in a practice who assumed the clientele of his retiring advisor one year before a bear market. He knew that he could cover his expenses even if he lost 30% of the clients in a flat market. Fortunately, he retained the clients, but the largely fee-based practice revenues fell 30% because of a bear market. Clearly, the 30% buffer was a wise precaution.

The upcoming "Transitioning Your Clientele to Your Successor" part of this book outlines what I think can be done to maximize the success of a transition between advisors, including factors affecting the compensation value of the referrals.

PART TWO: Transitioning Your Clientele to Your Successor

"The measure of a good manager is how the business performs after they leave."
—quote from a long-time client

In this section of the book, I will tell you what I think can be done to successfully transition a retiring advisor's practice to one or more successors. Your successors may or may not be part of your team before you start the transition process. I will also explain how my team and I successfully transitioned my practice to my two successors. Although my successors were part of my team, I believe that most of what I learned from the process will apply to all transitions.

You have worked hard to serve your clients, build your practice and build a good reputation. Your retirement transition should allow you to leave your career with peace of mind and the feeling of a job well done. As an advisor, you are a leader for your clients and a leader for your team. A good leader leaves an operation with a successor who can carry on seamlessly such that the leader's (in this case, the advisor) disappearance is almost unnoticed. For me, a job well done meant that my clients would be happy and well served long after I left the business. It also meant that my clients and I were confident that my successors would be able to guide them through whatever the financial future would bring. This will mean adjusting the investments and the service model to match changing circumstances and needs, but always keeping the overriding principles in place. My goal throughout my career was to help my clients reach their financial objectives while both the client and I maintained peace of mind. Over the years, my goal remained the same; however, the tools have evolved and expanded over time as our industry has changed and the use of technology has grown.

You will need to feel that you have chosen the right time to retire for you personally. Once you have set your retirement date, which may or may not be years away, it is very important to start laying the groundwork. A truly successful retirement transition will please all of those affected by your retirement (the stakeholders). The most important decision you will make is choosing your successor(s).

The successful retirement transition of a financial advisor requires careful planning, often over several years leading up to the day the advisor completely leaves their practice. I prepared clients for the transition for years in advance by mentioning during client meetings that the associate serving them would take over from me if I was "hit by a bus." I began looking at the potential valuation of the practice about two years before my expected retirement date and began seriously discussing it with my associates at that time. It is quite possible that these discussions triggered my most senior associate's thoughts about leaving. To his credit, his departure date gave the other two associates about 1.5 years to establish stronger relationships with the clients he had been serving. Clearly, the sooner you start serious discussions, the sooner the potential successor advisor can start seriously thinking about what they are taking on, and if it suits them.

The evidence shows that our succession plan worked and that my successors have succeeded in serving my clients well. The combined practices of my two successors retained 99% of the households after one year. This is essentially the same annual retention rate for my practice over the years. According to a survey by Price Matrix Insights (Stay or Stray white paper), annual retention rates for all advisors (not just those in the midst of retirement succession) ranged from 90-93% from 2009-2013.

Also, we received almost $10 million of new assets from clients between the date of my initial announcement and actual retirement. My successor's practices received additional deposits of over $22 million from my old clients and their referrals during the first 12 months after I retired.

History of Practice Transitioning in the Financial Advisory Industry

In the late 1980s, I observed the following about our industry's approach to the end of an advisor's career. When advisors retired, their clientele was disbursed amongst other advisors in the branch/firm with very little introduction to the succeeding advisor. The advisor was not paid referral compensation for their clientele. In many cases, the advisor was not involved in choosing their successor.

The result was that advisors would leave their firms of many years to go to the competition so that they could be paid for their practice. The advisors would bring the majority of their clients with them to the new firm. The process of moving the clients to a new firm was very time-consuming and likely stressful for the advisor. The change was disruptive for the clients, and the advisor's original firm would lose many clients.

Clearly this approach was the ultimate lose-lose situation. All stakeholders in the advisor's practice suffered.

In the 1990s, to avoid the loss of advisors and their valuable clientele, firms began to allow retiring advisors to refer their clientele to successors of their choice within the firm for compensation. This compensation was funded by the successor advisor. Over time, firms became more involved in the process, recognizing that smooth transitions to successor advisors within the firm benefited all of the stakeholders in an advisor's practice.

The Stakeholders of Your Retirement Transition

The benefits of the "win-win" approach are extremely evident during the retirement transition phase of an advisor's career. The groundwork for a successful retirement transition will have been laid by the successful implementation of the win-win approach throughout your career while you built your clientele, your team and your service model. You will have created a strong level of trust between all stakeholders in your retirement transition. I have identified five sets of stakeholders in the retirement transition of an advisor's practice below:

1) The clients (by far and away the most important of all stakeholders)

2) The successor advisor(s)

3) The remaining team members of the retiring advisor (excluding successor(s) if successors were part of the team, and excluding retiree team members who will not continue with the successor's team)

4) The advisor's firm

5) The retiring advisor and their family

I strongly believe, that in order to maximize the benefits for you (the advisor), the other four stakeholders should be winners and need to feel like winners upon completion of the retirement transition process. It might seem overly ambitious and altruistic to try to please all these stakeholders; however, ultimately, you the advisor will benefit greatly by doing precisely that. The size of the "pie" (the compensation for the referral of your clientele) will be greater and you will have peace of mind. The satisfaction of each of the stakeholders is generally very dependent on the satisfaction of the other stakeholders. If the client chooses to leave, everyone loses. If the successor advisor fails to please the clients, at the very least the client will not give additional business or referrals to the successor and once again everyone loses. If team members become less effective or choose to leave, client service and advisor efficiency will be adversely affected and once again, everyone loses.

Transition Stakeholders' Needs
I have listed below what I believe each of the stakeholders need to be winners and feel like winners in the transition process. By recognizing and appreciating these needs and striving to fulfill as many as possible, you will maximize your referral compensation and provide more peace of mind to all stakeholders. All practices and clienteles are unique, so the ability to meet these needs will vary. Your efforts to build your business and your planning for transition should position you to meet as many of these needs as possible.

Clients' Needs
- feel valued as the unique individuals they are by both the retiring advisor and the successor advisor
- believe the successor advisor understands and cares about them
- believe the successor advisor is well qualified to be their advisor (combination of education and experience)
- understand and feel comfortable with the future approach to investing and servicing of their accounts
- feel comfortable with the team supporting the successor advisor
- believe that the successor advisor will be there for them for many years into the future

The Successor Advisors' Needs
- be confident that they will be able to keep and please most of the retiring advisor's clients

- be able to live up to clients' expectations regarding level of service (amount, method and quality of contact including review meetings, financial plans, etc.)
- have complete confidence in the future approach to investing (maintaining the approach of retiring advisor or know that the clients will be comfortable with the successor's different approach)
- know that the firm supports the transition and will offer ongoing support to the practice
- believe they are paying a fair price for the referrals
- know the level of lifestyle they can maintain while they are paying for the referrals (We prepared our own sensitivity analysis to estimate the successor advisor's take-home pay while paying for the referrals.)
- be prepared to assume the leadership role of the resulting team that will serve the referred clients

Remaining Team Members' Needs
- believe they still have good career opportunities (likely within the successor's team)
- understand and are comfortable with their roles/ responsibilities during transition and after succession
- understand their compensation structure (salary and bonus) during transition and after succession
- know and are comfortable with their title after succession
- feel valued by the successor advisor (role, compensation, and title as well as personal attention will help)

Advisors' Firm Needs
- believe that the successor advisor is qualified (education, licences, and experience)
- have confidence in the successor's ability to keep the clients

- be confident that the successor advisor will stay with the firm
- believe that the successor advisor is not a compliance risk

Retiring Advisor's Needs
- feel they can trust the successor advisor(s) to take good care of the clients (investment advice, financial planning, overall service)
- feel they can trust the successor advisor(s) to value each team member appropriately and work well with the remaining team members
- believe they are receiving fair value for the referral of their clientele
- know that the firm supports the transition and will offer ongoing support to the successor advisor(s)

Satisfying the Needs of All Five Stakeholders
Satisfying the needs of all stakeholders will increase the compensation value of the referral of your clientele and give everyone peace of mind. It should be clear from the lists of needs above that the most important decision is choosing the successor advisor. However, the timing of your retirement and the execution of a well-thought-out plan is also extremely important. The next section outlines the various steps often involved in the transition of clients between advisors.

Steps of Transition

I believe the following steps will help to maximize the success of the transition of clients between advisors. Comments and details relating to each step follow the list.

1) Clarify or review your commitment to your clients.

2) Prepare a document clearly articulating your existing business model.

3) Review your service model to determine your preferred future approach for your successor to employ in each major service category:

   a) client communication

   b) selecting investments

   c) financial planning

   d) services relating to tax returns and tax strategies

4) Determine if you are willing and able to share your processes for delivery of services/products and practice management with your successor.

5) Determine the best future fee structure for your clientele.

6) Determine if you need a separate successor advisor for groups of clients in different geographic locations.

7) Choose your successor(s).

8) Plan a timeline for the remaining transition steps.

9) Compare service/product differences between the successor and the referring advisor.

10) Determine the future of the retiree team members.

11) Plan the roles of the successor's future team members including members from the retiree's team.

12) Start the process of creating contract(s) between the referring advisor, successor and firm.

13) Review or create a website and marketing materials.

14) Plan the office space.

15) Prepare scripts for conversations with your clients.

16) Notify your clients of your intention to retire (or refer the clients without retiring, if that is the case).

17) Plan and provide a period of overlapping service to your clients.

18) Notify your clients of your final retirement/referral date.

To help advisors organize their transition plan, I have created a Steps of Transition Timeline checklist, available as a free download from my website. This checklist facilitates the setting of target dates for the 18 steps including completion dates and space for notes relating to each item on the list.

Steps of Transition Comments and Details

1) Clarify or review your commitment to your clients.
Many advisors will have already articulated their commitment to clients; however, I was surprised to realize that I had never really written down my commitment to my clients. Reviewing your commitment will help you choose a successor with the same priorities. My overall commitment to my clients was to help them achieve financial peace of mind. My detailed commitment to clients can be found in the beginning of the Appendix of this book. Other examples of advisor commitments may be finding unique investment opportunities, seeking the highest possible returns or maximizing tax savings.

2) Prepare a document clearly articulating your existing business model.
Many older advisors will have modified their business model in their head over the years, but most have not written it down. A written business model will describe a practice's clientele and include the methods of client contact, the approach to investing and financial planning and how clients are charged. To enable advisors to create this document with minimal cost and effort, my website offers a checklist process to help advisors quickly identify most if not all aspects of their business model. I have provided all of the checklists in the form of a fully completed sample including the resulting summary in the Appendix of this

book. The checklists and related macros will allow a quick comparison to another advisor's business model to identify similarities and/or differences. A comparison of the retiring and potential successor advisors' practices written business models should help the retiring advisor choose the right successor. The right successor will not necessarily have the same business model as the retiring advisor but will have the business model that the retiring advisor believes will be best for the future. My handbook *Business Models for Financial Advisors* discusses all aspects of various business models in more detail.

3) Consider the best future approach to services.

Review the services portion of your business model. The services and products that you think are best for your clients going forward may or may not be exactly the same as you have provided in the past. My team and I determined that our current service model was the best for the immediate future, although I do expect my successors' services to evolve with technology, client preferences and the constantly changing world we live in. Non-team member successors are less likely to have or retain the exact service model as the referring advisor.

a) **client communication:** The retiring advisor's business model should identify the contact methods, reminders and personal touches that their clients are accustomed to and which of those should be continued by the successor advisor. Such services may be online meetings, driving to the client's home, providing regular newsletters, greater use of e-mail, Facebook, Twitter, etc.

b) **selecting investments:** The investment strategy that you think is best for your clients going forward may or may not be exactly the same as you have provided in the past. Stock picking versus managed money? Discretionary? More U.S. or international exposure? Use of different investment products or asset classes? My team and I determined that our current approach to investing would still be the best for our clients in the future, and I can see that they have maintained that approach through the appropriate modifications of my own accounts.

c) **financial planning:** There are many aspects to financial planning service that an advisor could choose to include or exclude from their offering (year by year forecasts, goal setting, retirement planning, estate planning, etc.). The retiring advisor needs to identify the financial planning services their clients are accustomed to and which services should be continued or added by the successor advisor.

d) **services relating to tax returns and tax strategies**: There are many different potential levels of an advisor's involvement in a client's tax return and strategies (tax return prep, gathering of tax information, formulating tax strategies, etc.). The retiring advisor needs to identify the tax related service the client is accustomed to receiving from the advisor and/or their team so there are no surprises in the first tax season after the transition to the successor advisor.

4) **Consider how willing and able you are to share your processes.**
An advisor may have developed many processes, presentations and systems to help them deliver many of their services/ products and to manage the practice. The advisor needs to decide which of these they wish to share with their successors. Such processes, presentations, etc. may add value to the group referral.

5) **Determine the best future fee structure.**
The retiring advisor may believe the client's costs should be more fee-based going forward, instead of transaction/ commission based. We had already converted most of our clients to fee-based and felt that was the best structure going forward for most of our clients.

6) Determine if a separate successor advisor is needed for clients in different geographic locations.

Are some of the retiring advisor's clients located far away from the advisor's current office? If so, the advisor should consider dividing the clientele between multiple successors based on physical location.

7) Choose your successor(s).

Choose a successor who will be able to take care of your clients the way you want them to be taken care of, keeping in mind the conclusions you reached in the preceding six steps. Based on those conclusions, you may decide that multiple successors are needed based on different service requirements. For example, you may have some clients who will require common stock picking and others who are most suitable for managed money. Your successor may actually be more qualified and more able to provide the clients with what you think they need going forward. I have included a more detailed section regarding choosing your successor later in this handbook.

8) Plan a timeline for the remaining transition steps.

Both the referring and the successor advisor(s) will benefit from planning a timeline together for the remaining transition steps. The timeline will likely be modified for each step as the transition progresses but should provide both the successor and the referring advisor with targets and estimates of when each remaining step will occur.

9) Compare service/product differences between the successor and the referring advisor.

The transition would likely benefit by the listing and comparison of services provided by both the referring advisor and the successor advisor. This comparison should point out any services that the client is accustomed to and might have otherwise been missed by the successor as well as services offered by the successor advisor that will be new and beneficial to the client.

10) Determine the future of the retiree's team members.

Some of the retiree's team members may not be a good fit with the successor's future team for reasons of their own, or for the successor's reasons. The successor and the advisor need to work with each member of the retiree's team to determine who will be part of the successor's team.

11) Plan the roles of the successor's future team members including members from retiree team.

Once the successor's team is determined, the successor can start to plan the roles and duties of each team member with some input from the retiree. My team building handbook describes potential team member roles in its "team structure" section and provides an appendix of "Team Member Duty Lists." These lists are also provided on my website.

12) Start the process of creating contract(s) between the retiree, successor(s) and firm.

I have included a more detailed section regarding contracts later in this handbook.

13) Review or create a website and desired marketing materials.

The successor advisor(s) may or may not have a working website. An existing website will likely need to be modified to reflect new team members and/or services. It is important for the successor's new clients to see a website which is at least up to the standards of the retiring advisor. Ideally the successor's website should be better. I intend to provide some ideas on how to improve advisors' websites in the handbook for presentations and processes.

14) Plan the office space.

Will more space be required to accommodate a bigger or combined team? Does the successor advisor need to change branches? Renovations to existing space or creating a new team location often takes much longer than anticipated. Planning ahead will reduce disruptions.

15) Prepare scripts for conversations with your clients.

The scripts should introduce the new advisor and, if necessary, describe any expected changes to the approach to investing and service model. Refer to the "Process of Informing Clients" section of this book for sample scripts and more information on how I prepared, used and modified them during my own transition process.

16) Notify your clients of your intention to retire.

See "Process of Informing Clients" section of this book.

17) Plan and provide a period of overlapping service to your clients.

Clients should be comfortable with the idea of you not being there anymore before you "disappear." It is best to develop a relationship between your successor and your clients through a period of joint or overlapping service to clients. This can be accomplished through joint meetings and through successor advisor contacts directly with your clients providing various services. Overlapping service before retirement is easiest if your associate(s) are the successor(s). The inclusion of the appropriate associate in every one of my client meetings gave my clients more confidence in the ability of the associate to take over from me. The overlap can also occur after retirement where the successor retains the retiree on salary for a specified minimum period. A one-year overlap would provide one full-service cycle allowing the client to experience the continuation of the services through the successor advisor. If the successor will be moving the referred clients to a new investment or service approach, a longer overlap period is–recommended so that the clients can see that the referring advisor endorses the change, and they have an opportunity to appreciate what the successor brings to the table

The best overlapping is likely to occur when a retiring advisor's associate of many years is the successor advisor. However, even the best laid plans can go awry. I lost my most senior associate slightly more than 1.5 years before my retirement. His last day in the office was March 19, 2015. We started calling clients to announce my pending retirement in June 2016. I was still in the office until November 30, 2016, my actual retirement date, so the associates who would ultimately be my successors had time to build stronger relationships with the clients previously serviced by the associate who left. I had hoped for a longer overlap period, but it seems to have been enough time. The evidence is my successors' high retention rate. My clients had the added advantage of knowing that my successor had been a member of my team for many years before they began servicing them. The clients had spoken to them occasionally when they backed up their fellow associate. Additional familiarity was provided by the team picture on the annual Christmas card and website.

Some of my clients had already been meeting with the associates and their assistants without me in the room. I made sure to drop in on their last meeting before my retirement to say thank you and goodbye.

18) Notify your clients of your final retirement date.
It is hard to know your final retirement date at the beginning of the process. This notice should provide your clients with enough time for their final goodbyes (likely a month or two). I have included a copy of the final notice that I sent my clients at the end of this part of this handbook.

Choosing Your Successor

I have noticed over the years that every successful advisor in this business is somewhat unique in how they run their practice. You need to find a successor who will be compatible with your clients' expectations and needs. I have listed many potential attributes that you should consider when choosing your successor(s). It will be difficult to find a successor who scores high in all attributes. Your challenge will be in finding the successor who will serve your clients best in the long term. This may mean choosing a successor who will change the investment or service model (i.e., to managed money, global diversification, fee-based, etc.) if you think such a change is needed. This is your chance to encourage and endorse the change to the clients even though you will not be implementing the change yourself.

Personality

The clientele of a mature practice will likely reflect or be comfortable with the personality of the retiring advisor. Your judgement regarding a suitable personality of the successor is very important. Many studies have shown that clients stay with their advisor because they like them. If you don't truly like the successor advisor, it is quite likely that your clients won't like them either. Clearly, if you are soft-spoken with a gentle manner, your clients may not be comfortable with a louder more aggressive style.

> *"I also feel confident that you have turned your business over to a very competent and likeable individual and look forward to working with (successor advisor)."*
> —a quote from one of my long-time clients

Clearly "likeable" matters!

Industry qualifications

Your successor should have, at least, all the industry qualifications you have. The more designations the better! Any additional designations (Portfolio Manager, CFA®, CFP®, Life Insurance licence, option/derivatives licence, etc.) will add to your successor's credibility in your clients' eyes and may make up for what is likely to be less years of experience.

Age

I think clients need to believe your successor will be there for at least ten years after you leave, but longer is better. Our clients were happy to know that they would have an advisor they knew and trusted for at least another 20 years as both of my successors were under 40. The clients who were over 60 years old were especially relieved that they would not have to find a new advisor in their senior years. A friend of mine told me that she would "never refer someone to an advisor who was within five years of retirement." Regardless of the successor's age, the successor must exhibit a level of personal maturity that clients will respect and be comfortable with.

Experience

I recommend at least five years of financial advice industry experience, but more is better for most successors. A successor with less than 10 years' experience should possess substantial compensating qualifications such as a previous professional career (e.g. accounting or law) or an overwhelming compatibility based on the other attributes listed in this section. The value of the potential successor's years of experience should be measured by more than just years. Is the advisors experience relevant to the investment strategy and services the successor is expected to provide to the retiree's clients? For example, an advisor whose experience is focused on stock picking and option strategies is likely not the best successor of a practice using a conservative, multi-manager managed money strategy even if they have over 10 years experience. Likewise, an advisor whose experience is focused on a conservative managed money strategy is likely not the best advisor to take over a practice with an investment strategy of stock picking and options. I also believe that more experience is preferable for a sophisticated clientele with complicated financial situations.

Pre-existing relationship
A successor with a pre-existing relationship with the retiree's clients is best but not always possible.

Keep your support staff
Your clients will likely have comfortable relationships with your support staff. They will like the familiarity of continuing to work with the same support staff, minimizing the changes they need to adjust to.

Compatibility with the successor's business model
In order to choose the right successor, the retiring advisor needs to review the potential successor's business model and compare it to the business model the retiring advisor believes will best suit their clients going forward. This is most easily done if the successor advisor and the retiring advisor have both articulated their business model in detail as shown in the Appendix and downloadable from my website. I will now discuss some major portions of the business model where I think compatibility is most crucial.

Existing client base of the potential successor
Does the potential successor have a client base similar to the referring advisor? Do the clients come from similar walks of life? Do they have similar personalities, goals and expectations?

Client communication
Your successor should be committed to continuing the past level of contact with each client at least until that client and the successor advisor have established a new agreed upon approach to contacts going forward. In general, your successor should

either like the amount and methods of contact you have provided to your clients or see ways to improve the service that you can support. Your successor must be willing to continue to provide those services that you know are most important to your clients. For example, our clients never heard voicemail when they called our office. Upon my retirement, many clients commented that they were happy to hear the "no voicemail during office hours" rule would continue.

Approach to investing

Will the successor advisor want to change all the investments? Will there be tax consequences for changes? Can the retiring advisor support those changes? An advisor I know told me that his approach is so unique that his successor will have to be a team member. It is possible that you believe a change in the approach to investing is warranted (for example, a change to discretionary management, using money managers or diversifying more globally). The successor you choose should agree with your expectations of the future. You will need to agree on the timing of transitioning the clients to any new approach to investing. The transition will be more effective if the retiring advisor is present and fully supportive of the new approach with the new advisor and the client.

Use of financial plans

The successor advisor needs to be able to continue providing whatever financial plans and financial planning services the referred clients had received in the past and more if possible.

Approach to fees

Are your clients used to paying commissions on transactions or fees based on asset value? What do you think will be best going forward? The successor you choose should agree with your expectations of the future. You will need to agree on the timing of transitioning the clients to the new approach to fees. The transition will be more effective if the retiring advisor is present with the new advisor and the client, fully supporting the new approach.

Segmented clientele

Many advisors have segmented their clientele into A,B,C,D clients based on size or other criteria, with different service models for each segment. An advisor may wish to choose different successors for different segments of their book. I have created a separate checklist tool to allow an advisor to articulate the business model of each segment. The appendix of this handbook provides a fictitious sample of this checklist tool for a segmenting advisor's client communication service model. The segmenting checklist tool is available on my website.

Overall, clients usually want to hear that the successor advisor will be able to continue the exact service they are accustomed to, with some potential improvements. The retiring advisor needs to be able to fully endorse whatever improvements the potential successor advisor would want to implement. The trusted retiring advisor's validation of the successor's improvements will show clients how they will personally benefit from the transition to the successor advisor. If you have prepared a document clearly articulating your existing business model as suggested in the previously mentioned steps of transition, you will have a ready-made list of services that you provide. You will also have considered what services you would like your clients to receive from your successor. This document and knowledge will help you choose a successor who is able and willing to provide such services.

Location in relation to clients

My successors lost two households immediately because the clients lived very far away, even though they had pre-existing relationships. These losses for geographic reasons remind me of a discussion I had with another advisor approaching retirement. The advisor was considering separating a group of clients located in another city from the rest of his clientele and choosing a different successor advisor located in that city. I think this is wise and should be considered in cases where a significant portion of the practice is located far away from the advisor's home branch.

Financial stability

Your successor must be able to fund the group referral compensation through their pre-existing practice and wealth or through the income from the referred clientele. The successor's personal finances should be able to withstand some loss of revenue from the referred clientele. The referral price and payments by successor sections of the referral compensation contract can be designed to minimize the impact of lost or irregular revenue as discussed in the upcoming contract section. A successor will have difficulty focusing on the clients if they are facing personal financial difficulty. The ultimate failure of a transition occurs when the successor leaves the business because the practice fails to support the successor's lifestyle.

I have created a Potential Successor(s) Evaluation Worksheet to help retiring advisors summarize and compare qualities of potential successors. This worksheet is available as a free download from my website.

My successors

In my case, the successor advisors were the two associates who were working with my clients at the time of my retirement. As a result, they both scored very high in all of the attributes mentioned above and had already proven to be very compatible with the clients.

My most senior successor was 35 years old and had been part of my team for 12 years (10 of those as an associate). My other successor was 31 years old with just under eight years on my team (3.5 of those as an associate). Thirty-one may sound too young and probably is in most cases. However, unlike most of my entry level hires, he was committed to a career as a financial advisor from a very early age and had already passed an industry course and spent two summers working in the financial industry at another firm, before I hired him upon graduation from university. His experience was extremely relevant as all those years were spent working with me on my team, and the clients all knew him well.

My successors both provided me with the peace of mind that comes with knowing that all my clients would be well looked after upon my retirement and for many years to come.

Client Transition Contracts

The successor advisor and the retiring advisor should both feel like they are getting a good and fair deal (win-win). In my opinion, the contract between the successor and the retiring advisor is best when all parties (successor advisor, retiring advisor and firm) share the risk of the future practice. The successor will be willing to pay more. The retiring advisor will receive more and be motivated to assist with a smooth transition. The firm is motivated to facilitate the transition fairly and efficiently to maximize retention of the clients and protect the reputation of the firm. It is very important that the retiring and successor advisors do not feel like adversaries in the negotiations over the compensation value of the referrals. An adversarial relationship will cause tension that may become evident to a client, harming the client's relationship with both advisors. A non-adversarial relationship will allow everyone to relax and focus on the real task at hand: retaining and pleasing the clients. This win-win approach will once again result in everyone's prosperity and peace of mind.

To prevent damaging our relationship, the successor advisors and I agreed to rely on our firm's management team to determine the value of the referrals and provide the template for the contract. The firm benefits by being fair to both the retiring and successor advisors. The firm will want to please the retiring advisor to encourage other aging advisors to think about retiring before their practice begins to shrink as the advisor winds down their career. No one benefits if an advisor is forced to retire for health reasons or dies before the transition can be fully planned and implemented. Firms are very aware of the current high average age of advisors and are motivated to reduce the risk of losing the clients of these aging advisors. The firm also wants to discourage the advisor from moving to a competing firm late in their career and taking their clients with them. The firm wants to keep the clients with an advisor who can maintain and grow the practice. The firm will want to please the successor advisor to establish/maintain a good relationship going forward.

It is surprising how long it takes to finalize the details of the contract(s). If you are lucky, your firm will have created a template for the contracts as well as a template for the valuation of a practice. However, you will still need to work out the details regarding the price, the payment frequency, the length of payment period, etc. You will need approval not just from yourself and the successor advisor(s) (and your respective lawyers) but also from various levels of your firm's management.

You will need a lawyer to either provide a contract or review a contract provided by your firm. A comprehensive listing of all of the possible inclusions in a contract is likely impossible and certainly beyond the scope of this book. The purpose of this section of the book is to give you the benefit of my personal experience and some of my conversations with others. Before working with a lawyer, it will help both the advisor looking to retire and potential successors to familiarize themselves with the issues that should be addressed by the contract(s) relating to the transition of the clientele.

Issues to be Addressed by Client Transition Contracts

a) Determining fair compensation for referring clientele

b) Referral compensation price: fixed or variable

c) Treatment of referrals

d) Firm guarantee of payments to the retiree and their heirs

e) Retiree and successor payment structures: frequency, duration and amount

f) Transitioning support required from retiree

g) Restrictions on retiree (non-compete)

h) Successor restrictions

i) List all referred households and accounts

When determining the fair compensation for the referral of a clientele, you are attempting to predict the future revenue stream for the successor advisor. Many factors relate to the specific clientele and some factors relate to all clienteles.

a) Determining Fair Compensation for Referring Clientele

Factors affecting the referral compensation for a specific clientele:

- The age of the clientele.

- The average assets per client household.

- The average revenue generated per client household.

- The total revenue produced by the clientele: should probably include an average of previous three years to account for market fluctuation (if retiring advisor has recently converted from transaction-based to fee-based, a greater emphasis should be placed on the most recent year of revenue)

- The revenue calculation should exclude clients who have transferred out during the period of the calculation of the average annual revenue.

- The revenue calculation should exclude one-time (non-recurring) revenue like life insurance purchases where the revenue is paid upfront and not recurring.

- Recurring fee-based revenue (discretionary accounts, mutual fund trailers and separately managed accounts with independent money managers) should bring a higher value than non-recurring transaction-based commissions simply because it is more predictable and reliable

- A practice including specific security selection (stocks, etc.) by the retiring advisor may carry a lower price because the client's confidence may not be transferable to the new advisor.

- Using independent money managers (mutual funds or separately managed accounts) allows the clients to maintain confidence in their investment strategy if the successor keeps the same managers and therefore adds to the value of the referrals.

- I believe that large sophisticated clients will be harder for the successor to retain as these clients often have other contacts in our industry. Consider inserting a contract clause reducing compensation for the risk of losing specific clients whose revenue is a large percentage of the practice.

- If the retiring advisor is unable or unwilling to provide a lot of assistance during the transition, the referring advisor's compensation should be lower (i.e. retiring advisor's health issues preventing an overlap of service).

External factors affecting the referral compensation for all clienteles:

- The financial advisor industry has compensated referring advisors very differently over time, ranging from approximately 1 to 2.5X revenue. The fluctuations have been caused by competitive factors, stock market conditions and various approaches to deferred compensation (restricted share plans, etc.).

- The pace of regulatory and industry changes seems to have accelerated in recent years requiring more nonrevenue generating work for firms and advisors.

- Many firms have reduced advisor payout percentages.

Some of the factors above can be easily identified and quantified. However, many factors can't be quantified or predicted. The retention of some clients will be beyond the control of the successor. Even the more predictable fee-based revenue is partially dependent on the unpredictable financial markets. Realistically the "fair" price of the referrals probably lies within a range. The successor may wish to reduce the referral compensation to allow a buffer for these uncertainties.

The agreement on the specific price within the range will be affected by the choice between assigning a fixed or variable price to the group referral.

b) Referral Compensation Price: Fixed or Variable

Fixed Price Contracts
A fixed price contract will set a compensation price for the group of referrals on the day the transition begins with no adjustments relating to future revenue or client retention. This is the simplest approach, providing relative certainty to the retiree and leaving all of the risk with the successor. The fixed price contract provides no financial incentive to the retiree to assist in the

transition. It does not foster a win-win relationship and might lead to a more adversarial relationship between retiree and successor. As a result, the price will likely be in the lower end of the range mentioned earlier.

Variable Price Contracts

A variable price contract will include a reduction in the total referral compensation price if certain revenue targets are not achieved by the successor. The target will likely be a percentage of an average of the practice's historical revenue.

I believe the contracts should provide financial incentives to maximize client retention. Both the retiring advisor and the successor advisor should be rewarded if the transition is successful. Conversely, if the transition does not go smoothly and revenue is significantly lower than expected, the retiring advisor's compensation should be reduced. In my opinion, the first two years will be an excellent indicator of the success of the transition. In a smooth stock market, I think a revenue retention rate of 80% after two years is a reasonable valuation target. Some firms will also include a second valuation date. If the transition does not go well, the successor advisor(s) and the firm will not earn as much as they expected. Payouts to all stakeholders will depend on the success of the ongoing practice.

Tax Considerations

Choosing between fixed and variable price contracts may affect the timing of the retiree's total taxes payable over the years. The Canada Revenue Agency (CRA) has rules to discourage deferring income over long periods of time. As I understand it, payments in a variable contract dependent on future revenue are unknown, and therefore unlikely to be considered deferred income. As a result, the payments can be spread over a longer period of time without adverse tax consequences. Payments for a fixed price contract may be limited to three years to avoid issues with the CRA. I am not a tax expert and recommend that a tax expert be consulted to clarify the tax consequences of the payment structure alternatives before a contract is agreed to.

c) Treatment of Referrals

If the arrangement between the retiring advisor and the successor advisor includes the calculation of future revenues, the contract should also include the treatment of revenues generated by future referrals from the referred clients. I expect there are many potential definitions of referrals. The written agreement of precise definitions is important in order to prevent future potential disagreements. Some examples of these definitions are shown below:

- Family member of referred clientele household in Retiree Agreement (RA) appendix: all such referrals should be added to the Successor Advisor Agreement (SAA) code so that they will count toward the valuation targets.

- Non-family member of referred clientele household on RA appendix: all such referrals should be added to the SAA code for the first two years.

- Referral from first referral where first referral was received after advisor retired: all such referrals should not be on the SAA code.

- Referral from retiring advisor after retired: all such referrals should be added to the SAA code so that they will count toward valuation targets.

d) Firm Guarantee of Payments to the Retiree and Their Heirs

In many transitions, the firm will act as a guarantor for payments to the retiree. This involves at least two separate contracts:

- A contract between the retiree and the firm
- Contracts between the firm and each successor

The contracts place the firm between the retiring advisor and the successor advisor.

The Firm's Contract with Retiring Advisor
When the firm acts as a guarantor, the firm pays the retiring advisor a guaranteed fixed monthly or quarterly amount for a specified period based on the contract's stated value of the referrals. The payments would change under a variable price contract if the group of referrals is revalued because the revenue targets are not met. Usually guaranteed payments would continue to the retiree's heirs should the retiree pass on before the contract is fulfilled.

The Firm's Contract with Successor Advisor
The firm deducts amounts from the successor's pay cheque based on the payment structure described in their contract with the successor. Similar to the retiree contract, the total amount of the payments would change under a variable price contract if the group of referrals is revalued because the revenue targets are not met.

The firm guaranteed retiree contract clearly gives the retiring advisor and their heirs more security. I would argue that separate contracts also protect the successor. I expect a retiree would be less tempted to breach the non-compete clause of a contract with a large institution than with an individual.

Providing the guarantee gives the firm more control over the choice of the successor, the price of the practice and the transition time period. This control allows them to protect the clients, the firm's reputation and the future revenue streams for the firm. The firm's payments to the retiree often coincide with the successor payments so the firm is effectively cash flow neutral.

The firm would clearly act as the administrator of the guaranteed contract deducting the successor's payments from their pay cheque. The retiree receives their payments from the firm and does not need to collect them directly from the successor.

Non-guaranteed transitions would require one contract directly between the retiree and each successor. I believe the firm for a non-guaranteed contract could still act as the administrator by deducting payments from the successor's pay cheque and passing on the payment to the retiree.

e) Retiree and Successor Payment Structures: Frequency, Duration and Amount

Payment structures vary among firms and even within firms themselves. They need to be structured so that the retiree, the successor and the firm are all comfortable. The retiree and the successor's circumstances can vary greatly in every transition. If the firm is not guaranteeing the retiree payments, the schedules for the retiree payments and the successor payments will match completely. If the firm is guaranteeing the payments, the two payment schedules can be quite different unless the firm wishes to be immediately and continuously cash flow neutral.

Payments to the Retiree
Some retirees are more dependent on the income from the transition than others. Most retirees would like consistent monthly or quarterly payments. Many retirees would like to be paid out as quickly as possible. Others would rather be paid out over a longer period, possibly to reduce taxes or for the potential of receiving more for the practice under a variable price contract.

Payments from Successors
In order for a transition to be successful, the successor needs a sustainable income to fund their lifestyle while they pay for the retiree's clientele referral. If the successor advisor already has an established practice funding their lifestyle, the payment

structure has less of an impact on them. If the successor is an associate from the retiring advisor's team, their only income will be from the referred clientele. They will likely need a longer payment period and will be more concerned with a volatile pay cheque.

The volatility of the successor's take-home pay can be reduced when the successor's ongoing payments are a percentage of the referred clientele's revenue for the corresponding period (instead of a flat monthly amount). The successor advisor will avoid empty pay cheques on low revenue periods and will pay off the transition faster in high revenue periods. All the stakeholders lose if the successor is forced to leave the business because the cash flow after transition payments is too low to fund the successor's lifestyle. Forcing clients to transition to yet another advisor, especially during a bear market, could harm clients' confidence in the firm and will likely result in a loss of clients. This percentage of revenue payment approach might cause temporary imbalances in cash flow for the firm (payments to retiree exceeding payments from successor), especially if the stock markets suffer losses soon after the transition date. I think firms should be willing to accept this imbalance until the end of the transition, especially for the successor advisors coming from the retiring advisor's team.

Unfortunately, some firms require periodic "realignments" where they will deduct additional amounts from the successors' pay cheque to catch up when the firm's total payments to the retiree exceed total payments received from the successor. I think these "realignments" are harmful to the associate taking over their retiring advisor's practice and could result in mostly older advisors taking over retiree's practices, resulting in a further consolidation of client assets with aging advisors. This puts the firm's future revenue at risk and may result in the loss of associates who should be the future advisors for the firm.

In my opinion, the contract between the firm and the successor should also provide the successor with protection from changes the firm could impose on the advisor's share of future revenue (often referred to as compensation grids). I think it is unfair to expect a successor to pay a price for the referral group based on current payouts with no protection from potential pay-cuts controlled by the firm.

It is impossible to predict how clients will react to their advisor's retirement, and it is impossible to predict how the markets will affect future revenue. I think basing the successor advisor payments on a percentage of the revenue is a smart way to reduce the volatility of the successor advisor's paycheque. Reducing the volatility of the paycheque in this manner does not impact the total cost of the practice and does not reduce the successor's incentives.

f) Transitioning Support Required from Retiree

The contract should contain a clause outlining the timing of transitional support required of the retiree. If there is a strong pre-existing relationship between the successor and the clients, the contacting of clients and service overlap may have occurred before the retirement date. If so, the retiring advisor might leave on the commencement date of the transition contract (as I did). When the successor is not from the retiree's team, the successor often hires the advisor to stay on in a consulting capacity. This arrangement may or may not be included in the contract.

g) Restrictions on Retiree (Non-Compete)

The contract between the firm and the retiree will usually contain a non-compete clause to ensure the retiring advisor does not pursue the referred clients or team members. The retiree should make sure they understand the restrictions and how the restrictions relate to their future plans.

h) Successor Restrictions

The contract between the firm and the successor will likely demand a commitment from the successor to stay with the firm for the life of the contract.

i) List All Referred Households and Accounts

I also believe all contracts should include an appendix listing all households and accounts referred to the successor advisor.

— — —

In summary, for most transitions, I believe all of the stakeholders are best served by variable price contracts where the firm guarantees retiree payments and the successor payments are based on a percentage of revenue earned after transition.

Process of Informing Clients

You will have worked very hard to choose the right successor and to set them up in the best possible position to succeed with your clients. The whole point of a succession plan is to prevent clients from feeling the need to run off to another advisor that you have not chosen for them. Your process of informing clients should answer all the obvious questions they are likely to have when you give them your news.

Before you begin informing clients that you will be leaving, you must have several "ducks in a row."

1) You must be absolutely certain that you have chosen the right successor and that they are committed to taking good care of your clientele.

2) Your firm has agreed to the named successor(s).

3) Your successor(s) and your firm's management must have agreed to the basics of the transition contract(s) (formula for the practice valuation, payment method, etc.).

4) You should have an approximate date for your departure.

5) You need to know the plans for the remaining team members.

It was very important to us that each and every client heard the news directly from us via personal phone calls. Using the phone allows you to respond immediately to your clients' reactions, address any misunderstandings and put their minds at ease.

In the beginning, I was very nervous about calling the clients with my news. However, after a few calls, I relaxed as many clients told me that I deserved to retire after 33 years in a demanding career and that they appreciated all that I had done for them. Many of them told me how happy and relieved they were that they knew and had confidence in my successor.

Initial Notification Phone Call Lists

We created very complete lists of all the people we needed to call. The list grouped relationships together (families, referrals, clients who knew each other). We tried to call groups of related clients (families or referrals) within minutes of each other to minimize the likelihood of a client hearing about my retirement from someone else. I called each client with their associate (successor) on the phone with me. The calls averaged five minutes in length. It is important to take as long as each client needs to digest the news, ask questions and reminisce. The successor advisor took notes during each call and would update the list and our contact management system after each session of calls (call sessions ranged from 15 minutes to two hours). We had over 300 households to call, and it would have been impossible to keep track of who we had successfully reached without careful note taking. I highly recommend calling some mid-sized, affable clients first to provide you with some practice and to give you an opportunity to modify your script if necessary (benefiting from yet another opportunity to learn by listening to your clients).

Initial Notification Phone Call Script

The moment a client hears that you are retiring could be quite startling and emotional for them. The following questions will likely pop into their minds:

1) When exactly are you leaving?

2) Who is going to choose and watch my investments after you are gone?

3) Will the new advisor want to change the investments?

4) Who will answer my questions about financial matters (estate planning, life insurance, retirement planning)?

5) Who will make sure I stick to my savings plans (contributions to RESPs, RRSPs, TFSAs)?

6) Will service continue like before?

7) Will the successor advisor be in the same location?

8) What do you plan to do in retirement?

9) How long have you been my advisor?

These questions might cloud your client's minds so that they don't even hear the next couple of minutes of the conversation. You need to give them time to digest the news. You also need to answer the above questions, sometimes before they are asked, and then repeat the answers again later in the conversation to be sure that your answers registered. When the reminiscing starts, they will often ask you when they became your client. Your script should include answers to the questions you expect.

We started calling clients in June 2016 revealing the "expected" retirement date of November 30, 2016. We explained there were a lot of "i's to dot and t's to cross" before we finalized the date. We used a script for calling clients and revised it after several uses. When forced to leave a message, I said that (name of associate/successor) and I would like to talk to (name of client(s)) together, and that we preferred to speak with both spouses at the same time if possible. We also mentioned in the message, "It is all good, nothing to worry about, but please call us back as soon as possible," so they were not alarmed. (It was very unusual for both myself and my associate to call together and somewhat unusual to request both spouses on the same call.)

We asked every client to keep the news quiet until we notified them with a formal retirement notice. We discovered, while making the calls, that clients welcomed the request for confidentiality as they very much appreciated hearing the news directly from us with a personal phone call. Several clients mentioned other professionals (doctors, dentists, bankers and lawyers) who had retired without informing them. One client mentioned seeing their dentist of many years for a check up one week and the very next week received a letter in the mail informing them that he had retired and giving the name of the dentist who was taking over. The clients had never even met the new dentist. Another client reminded me that she had discovered that her lawyer had retired when she called his office to update her will (of which he was executor). Numerous clients have complained to us over the years about their bankers being replaced with no notice or introduction to the successor.

I strongly recommend preparing a script containing all the things you might need to say, starting with the most important. You will find yourself not getting through the whole script, and that is okay, as long as you cover the essential points. I have included a sample of our retirement phone call script. The script highlights the points I wanted to be absolutely sure of saying (confidentiality and thank you). It is easy to find yourself caught up in the conversation, reminiscing, etc. which often starts the second you say "retire." Also, emphasize that your successor is truly replacing you. If your successor is a member of your team, sometimes the client just hears they are continuing to be there and may not understand that the associate is truly taking over. Remember, they may be quite surprised and may be still digesting your news while you continue with your script. Be careful not to rush, and be sure to give them time to comment early in the conversation. You usually only touch the first few items on your script, but it is helpful to have all the other points there to refer to as appropriate during the conversation.

Clients' questions relating to the future should be answered by the successor. I included the successor on the call to allow the client to hear about the future directly from the person who would be providing the future service and advice.

We were very careful and thought we were very clear. However, we were still surprised by questions from some clients, sometimes days later, that indicated our message was not received correctly.

We gave the clients plenty of warning, so they did not feel any pressure. Many clients wanted to see me one last time before I retired. I think it is safe to say that all the clients were very grateful for the "heads-up." It helped that we were simply following through with the promise that I had made over the years, that the associate would take over.

The following sample script closely resembles the script we used to introduce clients to my retirement plans. Please note that my original script began by stating I would be retiring, probably by the end of the year. After several calls, we modified the script to begin with telling the client that my associate was taking over from me. This modification was made when we found that many clients would start reminiscing immediately upon hearing the word retirement, causing them to miss my next few comments about my associate taking over. By saying that my associate would be taking over first, we hoped to already have put the client's mind at ease when they heard the word retirement.

Sample Retirement Phone Call Script

Message left if phone not answered:
I am calling with (successor's name). We have some news. It is all good, nothing to worry about, but please call us.

Script if phone answered:

We are calling because I'd like you to know that I expect (successor's name) to be fully taking over for me probably before the end of the calendar year.

I will be 60 in October, and I would like to retire after 33 years of advising. I did my financial plan, and it looks like I will be OK.

(Successor's name) and our team will continue providing all the advice and service that you've come to expect from us from the same location we are in now.

I would like more time to spend with my husband and my teenage son, while he's still at home, and my 91-year-old mother. I am also thinking about writing a book about investing and another book about advising.

Please keep this news confidential because we want to be sure clients hear this directly from me (you never know who knows who). We will not tell other advisors in our firm until all my clients know, and this could take a few months because I am taking August off.

Thank you for being my client. You started with me back in _____, and I have enjoyed working with you.

(Your firm's name) has fully endorsed (successor's name) and my retirement plan.

The retirement plan provides you with continuity of service.

I have peace of mind knowing that you will be well looked after.

(Successor's name) has been on my team for over _____ years, (___ of those as an associate).

(Successor's name) is registered as a portfolio manager with our regulators.

He or she has been through __ bear markets, including the financial crisis.

(Successor's name) has helped with:

- Selecting our recommended managers (including offsite visits)
- Selecting stocks, bonds, mutual funds, etc. for recommendation to our clients
- Developing our unique financial plan
- Writing client letters
- Managing assets within our discretionary accounts program
- Improving our website
- Working with our life insurance experts
- Hiring and training new team members and other personnel issues

– Other duties showing successor is prepared to take over

(Successor's name) has a lot of experience in selecting managers, always participating in meetings with managers when they visit and also visiting managers on the road, (Here I gave the specific names of the managers and the cities my successors travelled to see them in their home offices.)

My two successors have told me that they will continue to work together going forward so that you maintain the benefits of a big team, no voicemail and someone knowledgeable will always be around.

Sample Formal Retirement Letter

When I had finalized my retirement date and we had reached all our clients, we sent them a formal retirement letter/e-mail a month before the final retirement date. I sent the letter as soon as everything was finalized. I used the opportunity to remind clients of the qualifications of my successors and to thank them once again. My final/formal retirement letter to clients is shown below.

November 1, 2016

Dear Client:

As you already know, I have decided to retire from my career as an Investment Advisor. As expected, my last day at work will be November 30, 2016. You, my clients, have made this a wonderful 33 years.

I am very pleased to leave my clients with my very capable associates and our team.

As you know, _____ will be your new Investment Advisor after my retirement. _____ has been working with me for over ___ years. He has excellent judgement and has proven himself to be very knowledgeable. It gives me peace of mind, knowing that _____ will be taking care of you and your financial needs going forward.

We expect that _____ name will appear as your Investment Advisor on your December 31, 2016 statements.

I've read and heard many times (from many of you) that retirement is not about doing nothing, but rather, it is about doing the things you have always wanted to do but were unable to find the time. I look forward to spending more time with my family.

I will also be attempting to write a couple of books. One book will be about investing and planning for individuals like yourselves. The other book will be for financial advisors. Hopefully I can put some of what I learned in 33 years into books that some people will want to read!

I must tell you that much of what I have learned has come directly from you my clients or from helping my team pursue answers to your very interesting questions.

Thank you for being my client all these years!

SIGNATURE

Final Thoughts on Transitioning to Your Successor

The Transition is Your Parting Gift to the Stakeholders of Your Practice

Clients will be grateful that you have taken the time to warn them about your upcoming retirement and introduce them to the next advisor. They will likely be especially grateful if they have had the opportunity to "groom" your successor through the associate path.

A small business couple told us that they really appreciated the continuity of service. They were very pleased that the associate they had been working with would be taking over from me because the associate was already very familiar with their situation. They reminded me that they had been referred to me years ago by the client's mother when they had complained about staff turnover with their current bank. They had been with one bank where they "suffered from continuous turnover," so they had changed to another bank. Two months later two different bankers were given to them and then two months later another new banker. "None of the bankers knew what was told to the previous banker." The client had to reexplain both their personal and business banking and investment goals and objectives to the new banker only to have the new banker changed again without notice. The client said, "It is amazing that the banking industry does not understand the client's desire for continuity! It is hard to have a long-term plan with constantly changing advisors."

I think most, maybe all, of my clients were very relieved that the associate they already knew was taking my place. One client said, "My heart fell to my feet," until we said my associate was taking over. I think I revised the script at that time to name my successor earlier in the conversation. A retired partner of a big accounting firm wrote, "(successor advisor) has been our main person for a number of years, and we are happy that he is taking over the helm."

A good transition to your successor is your final opportunity to do good things for your clients, your team and your firm. It is similar to a last will and testament. I have often said to clients, "Be very careful with your will. It will be the last words you ever say to your family/heirs, and it will be remembered forever." The last thing you do for your clients is provide them with your successor, and that successor will affect their financial lives for many years to come. It was my goal to provide them with peace of mind long after I left. I think I have accomplished this with the help of my successors, my team and my firm.

Enjoy the Transition Period

You may have as much as two years from the day you decide you are going to retire until the actual retirement date. Try to make the most of it. Recognize what you are giving up, and step back to allow yourself to appreciate these "joys of being an advisor," such as:

- Relationships with wonderful clients.
- Relationships with wonderful team members.
- Sharing your workspace with intelligent colleagues.
- The respect you enjoy from other industry participants (money managers, wholesalers, firm management, other advisors and team members).

Recognize and savour these benefits with extra appreciation and the realization that many of these joys may diminish or disappear when you retire.

PART THREE: The Retirement Exit Decision

Deciding when to retire is a very personal decision. I give my own reasons in "Why I Retired" as well as what I enjoy most about being retired. In "Hints That It May Be Time to Start Preparing for Retirement," I have provided a list of possible reasons for retiring that I have experienced or learned from others in the financial advice industry. I then point out many of the personal and business dangers of waiting too long to retire. Finally, I outline several steps that I recommend in preparation for an advisor's retirement.

As I became more confident in my decision to retire, I began to look forward to retirement so much that I began to wonder, "Why doesn't everybody want to retire right now?" I began to listen to other people's thoughts about retiring and concluded that the timing of one's retirement is an extremely individual and personal decision. We all have different priorities, different interests and different obligations as well as different financial situations. The right time for me to retire was unique to me and is clearly not the right time for everyone. I retired at 60 and am confident it was the right time for me. I spoke to a 90-year-old former advisor who had retired at the age of 72. After 18 years, he remains confident that 72 was the right age for him. We are fortunate in this industry that most of us can choose when we retire and can usually wait until we are fully prepared. I intend to provide you with ideas to help you fully prepare yourself and your practice for your retirement, whatever the timing you choose.

<u>Why I Retired</u>

There are many reasons why I retired when I did.

Age: As I approached the age of 60, I sensed the reality of getting older and how short life can be. Financial advising is a very demanding and stressful profession. Unfortunately, I have seen many people burn out in this business and some die young while still working. I often wondered when the individual would have retired had they known their own personal expiry date. I did not want to wait until I had health issues or suffered burnout.

Time pressure: Although I loved being an advisor and working with my team and clients, I was starting to feel pressured by the demands of the business even though I had delegated much of the day-to-day duties to my team. I was becoming frustrated with the lack of time to fully satisfy other interests and responsibilities. I felt I was always rushing to the next thing, rarely truly relaxing or taking time to enjoy what I was currently doing. I never seemed to have enough time for my 91-year-old mother, my teenage son, my wonderful husband or my friends and other family members. Honestly, I also wanted to spend more time doing things for myself like exercising almost every day, reading more books, puttering around my home and spending more time at the cottage. I wanted to stop feeling guilty when I spent time doing things solely for myself.

Desire to do other things: For years I have longed to write a book for clients and another for advisors. Upon retirement, I looked forward to being able to write these books without having to take time from my family or my clients. I love the financial advice business and hope to continue to contribute through these handbooks for advisors and a book for clients about achieving financial peace of mind. The book for clients will speak positively about the financial advice industry and show why clients benefit from and need financial advisors.

Practice readiness: Fortunately, thanks to how I built my practice, I was satisfied with my career accomplishments and was very happy with those taking over my practice (my successors).

Financially prepared: My financial plan indicated I could afford to retire and maintain the lifestyle I desired for myself and my family.

What I Enjoy Most About Retirement

Retirement gave me the freedom to relax and enjoy life. My responsibilities were greatly reduced, and I was free from the everyday demands of responding to client questions or needs. My days were no longer scheduled from start to finish, although I did develop a new routine.

Retirement has allowed me to enjoy more of the pleasures of my pre-retirement life:

-   More time to see my family and friends
-   Being home for dinner every night with my husband and son
-   "Date night" starts with a movie matinee and then dinner
-   Time to read (about 50 books in my first year of retirement)
-   Time to listen to more music and go to concerts
-   Regular massages
-   Midday shopping (no crowds, better service, have time to bargain shop)
-   More time at the cottage
-   Exercising almost every day

Retirement has also allowed me to start new projects. I have enjoyed finally being able to work on my lifelong goal of writing a book for advisors and a book for clients.

I have no regrets about retiring! By the time I finish this book, I will have been retired for over a year. I remain very pleased with the timing of my retirement.

Hints That It May Be Time to Start Preparing for Retirement

Retirement is an enormous change. We are therefore naturally afraid to hear the hints that are often right in front of us. You need to listen to yourself and the people around you. Below I have listed many personal and business reasons that may be an indication that it is time for you, the financial advisor, to consider retirement.

Personal Reasons
- You feel the need to spend significantly more time with your family.
- You are feeling that you don't have time to explore other interests.
- You are becoming frustrated with the lack of time for non-work-related activities.
- You are approaching conventional "retirement age."
- You are starting to feel like your friends are all retired or retiring, and you are becoming envious of their freedom.
- Your health is starting to suffer.
- If you were told you were sick and dying, would you wish you had retired earlier?

Business Reasons
- You find yourself thinking that advising used to be more fun but now it is feeling more like work.
- You have less patience for your clients.
- You have less patience for your staff.

- You have less patience for the demands of the industry (documentation, paperwork, etc.).

- You are more easily offended or bothered by client comments that make you feel unappreciated.

- You are finding negative movements of the stock market harder to undergo.

- You may feel that the business is changing so much that you don't want to put in the effort required to keep up (products, technology, services, etc.).

- You may believe that clients will now be best served by an advisor who is a qualified discretionary money manager, but you are not willing to take the courses or do what is required to become a discretionary money manager yourself.

- You may believe that fee-based accounts are the future for your business and have meant to convert your clients, but you don't want to spend the time and energy required.

I remember facing a situation a year or so before my retirement. I was conversing with the son of a recently deceased client who was acting as power of attorney for his widowed mother. He insulted my integrity, insinuating that we were not recommending ETF index funds solely because the fees were lower. He insisted that there was no valid reason for using money managers and that advisors recommending money managers were only doing so to receive higher fees. He was very insulting and disrespectful. I was very disappointed as his father had always been very aware of the fees and had been very appreciative of our service and advice. I did not say anything inappropriate, but I did lose my temper. I can't remember ever losing my temper like that with another client. Looking back, I am sure that I had more patience and a "thicker skin" a few years earlier. I remember thinking, "I should have had more patience. I should not have lost my temper, and maybe I should be retiring soon!"

The Dangers of Waiting Too Long to Retire

The ideal retirement age is not the same for everyone. Each individual and their circumstances are unique, but there are dangers that are inherent to everyone (the client, the advisor, the team and the firm) the longer they wait.

Personal Dangers
The older you are:

- the more your personal peace of mind may be affected by the stress of the many uncontrollable elements of the financial industry (markets, compliance requirements, firm policies).

- the more likely the stress of the business will directly affect your health.

- the more likely someone you care deeply for will develop health problems and require more of your attention/time causing you to rush the retirement transition process or prevent you from helping the loved one as much as you would like.

- the more likely that travelling or working on your "bucket list" will become more difficult.

- the more likely it is that the people you wish to spend more time with pass away.

A friend of mine retired very young, at 45, after a very successful career as a financial advisor. He developed terminal cancer in his early fifties with no earlier indications. Needless to say, he and his family were very grateful that he retired when he did, allowing him to spend more time with them and allowing him to clear his bucket list. Unfortunately, we never know how long we have.

Business Dangers

The older you are:

- the more likely your clients will start looking for their next advisor as they know how old you are. If you have not identified a clear successor, clients may feel the need to take action themselves before they consider themselves less capable of choosing a good advisor to replace you.

- the more likely you will develop a health problem that may cause you to rush the retirement transition process resulting in a less successful transition and reduction in compensation for the referral of your clientele to your successor. Your practice's "key person risk" increases with your age as the likelihood of your health failing increases.

- the less valuable your aging clients usually become to a successor.

- the less access you will have to your clients' next generation as they acquire their own advisors (unless they are already your clients).

- the harder it is for associates to stay interested and loyal to you especially if you have toyed with their future by changing or never really setting a retirement date.

- the less capable you likely become: A study by Michael Finke and Sandra Huston of Texas Tech University and John Howe of the University of Michigan found that as people age, the ability to answer basic financial questions that include knowledge and the ability to apply that knowledge gets worse. However, there is no corresponding loss in confidence in one's ability to make financial decisions. The researchers found that average financial literacy scores fell by half between the ages of 65 and 85. The rate of decline was the same after controlling for characteristics like education, gender and wealth. Clearly it is difficult for anyone to recognize reduced abilities in themselves. I think we owe it to our clients to monitor our own capabilities when we get older.

Many of the above business and personal reasons could very well result in your loss of effectiveness at work. If your skills, attitude or level of dedication deteriorate significantly, sooner or later you will be doing a disservice to your clients, your team and your firm. The referral value of your clientele will fall accordingly.

Steps Towards Retirement

I think some advisors delay retiring because they are stuck in the habits of their life and are reluctant to look outside their life's box. The timing for your retirement needs to work well for your clients, your team, yourself and your family. Keep in mind that retiring well as a financial advisor takes time to plan, even if you have a strong team in place. Preparation on many fronts is required to provide a comfortable transition for all of those affected by your retirement.

Prepare Yourself and Your Family Psychologically

You need to know what you will be doing with your time to deal with the loss of the daily structure and feeling of productiveness. Modifying your working hours, possibly years in advance of retirement, will help prepare you and your family for the change in daily home life brought on by retirement. I have listed several simple ways to modify your working hours. The best timing of these modifications will be unique to your family's lifestyle. I highly recommend taking more and more time away from the office, one way or another, in the years leading up to your retirement.

Ways to Modify Your Working Hours

- Stop working on weekends.

- Start going home at 5 o'clock. (I never really accomplished this.)

- Start coming into the office a little later in the morning. (I accomplished this happily and consistently.)

- Take one day off a week. (I took Fridays off for 12 years before I retired with very rare exceptions.)

- Take more vacation time.

Taking these steps to modify your working hours will give you a taste of how you will spend your time in retirement. At first, you may not know what to do with yourself and may find it difficult to unwind enough to truly enjoy the time. You may be tempted to quickly conclude that you are not even close to ready for retirement. I encourage you to commit yourself to several months of a new schedule. You will likely find yourself planning to fill your time with new pastimes or interests you forgot about. Try to be patient and allow yourself time to figure it out. It is time to seriously consider retiring when you have taken most or all of the above steps to modify your working hours and still don't have enough time to do the things you really want to do.

Prepare to Let Go of the Power and Status of Work Identity

A retiring advisor needs to be prepared to let go of the power and status of their work identity. When we are fully engaged in an active practice, our views are sought after by clients, peers and the firm's management as well as suppliers of investment products. Members of the industry are constantly showering us with attention and invitations, hoping to convince us to recommend specific securities or investment products to our clients . You may have several people working for you and are likely used to directing and delegating to a team. All of this adds up to you receiving a lot of attention and respect. Most of us take this attention and respect for granted and may not realize how much it affects our confidence and feeling of self-worth. Most of this attention and respect will likely disappear upon your retirement. We will all be affected differently based on our personal psyche. You will need to think about this and prepare yourself.

Consider the following quote from *The Retirement Maze: What You Should Know Before and After You Retire* by Rob Pascale, Louis H. Primavera, Rip Roach: "Working toward goals with others provides a sense of membership and acceptance in a group and being accepted by others helps people maintain their self-esteem. When this opportunity for social contact and group membership is reduced or cut off, as can occur in retirement, people can feel isolated and socially disconnected."

However, retiring does not have to mean ending relationships that have developed from your professional life. There may be relationships you wish to maintain. So... maintain them! Be the initiator! It is up to you who you maintain relationships with. I have spoken to many of my colleagues from my old firm and several clients as well. No one has refused to see or talk to me because I am no longer a practicing advisor. In fact, your former colleagues may appreciate your sympathetic and understanding ear. Maintaining relationships with colleagues after my retirement was, and is, very important to me. I did my best before I retired to let those people know that I hoped to continue a relationship after retirement. In time, you may have less in common with your former colleagues and will likely drift away from some of them as personal interests take them and you elsewhere.

Prepare Your Own Finances
You personally need to be financially able to retire, hopefully with the same lifestyle you and your family have been accustomed to plus a buffer, so your lifestyle will not be affected by volatile markets. Treat yourself like you would treat a client who is preparing for retirement. Prepare your own detailed financial plan with multiple possible scenarios regarding retirement date, returns on investments, potential spending, etc.

Prepare Your Successor

Your team or successor needs to be ready to take over. "Transitioning Your Clientele to Your Successor", part 2 of this book, discussed this topic in much greater detail. If your team will be taking over from you, modifying your working hours as mentioned above will help them adapt to your eventual full-time absence, similar to how the modified working hours will help you and your family adapt gradually to your future retirement.

Prepare Your Clients

Your clients need to be comfortable with the idea of your retirement and with the people who will be taking over from you. We had a succession plan roughly in place for many years before I retired. Essentially my succession plan was in place as soon as I assigned associates to developing their own relationships with specific portions of my clientele. I introduced clients to the succession plan by casually mentioning that "If I was hit by a bus, the associate sitting right here in the room with us would take over." I would make these comments during review meetings. Because I retired at a relatively young age, I was rarely directly asked when I was planning to retire, although it was starting to come up more in my last couple of years. I always answered the question honestly stating that I was not going to work forever, that I would give fair warning and that luckily for all of us the associate they were working with would take over.

In hindsight, I think my retiring at the age of 60 was good for my clients. I believe many clients felt that if I was just following my own advice as an advisor, being able to retire at age 60 was appropriate. I wonder how they would have felt if I retired at a much earlier age. Would they have wondered if I had overcharged them?

Final Thoughts on Considering When to Retire

Fortunately, in our business, we are exposed to the experiences of many clients preceding and after their retirement. As usual, we can learn a lot from listening to our clients. Many of your clients will have retirement resources similar to yours. In most cases, my clients provided good examples: disciplined exercise programs, travelling while healthy, developing other interests (taking courses and learning languages) and making the most of their time and freedom. Others raised warnings of retiring too early, retiring too late and what can go wrong during retirement.

A friend of mine gave me the book How to Retire Happy, Wild, and Free: *Retirement Wisdom That You Won't Get from Your Financial Advisor* by Ernie J. Zelinski — an interesting title for a book gift to a retiring financial advisor! The book provides many useful lists of literally hundreds of potential activities as well as many humorous and interesting thoughts regarding retirement and life in general. The lists may remind you of activities you always wanted to do or interests you wanted to pursue but have conveniently forgotten because you realized you did not have time for them while you were working. I expect the book will help you to start looking outside your "professional box" and allow you to envision what your happy and satisfying retirement could be like.

Epilogue: Three Years Later

As I write this epilogue, it is a little over three years from the time I retired. I can now look back at the book I wrote first (this handbook) with a fresh perspective and some hindsight regarding the consequences of my decisions.

I am happy to say that I still have no regrets. I am more certain than ever that the right timing for retirement is unique for every advisor. I am confident that the timing was right for me. My successors have proven that they were well chosen and have more than lived up to expectations. My successors have provided both my clients and me with peace of mind. Their success has also proven that our transition process was effective resulting in a win-win for clients, myself, my successors and the firm.

> *"Chris cared and continues to care about her clients - absolutely evident in her approach to her team and her solid plan for her retirement and the transition of her clients to the RIGHT advisors. The final proof is her two successors' very high client retention rate three years after her retirement."*
>
> —Wilma Ditchfield
> Senior management of a Big 5 Canadian Bank

My life is still extremely full. I am enjoying the freedom and flexibility to do many of the things I have always wanted to do now that I have the time. My mother is 95 now, and I am grateful that I have had more time to spend on her care without the conflict of a full-time practice. I have thoroughly enjoyed having more time for my husband and son. I have enjoyed many "movie-matinee dinner dates" with my husband. I have maintained many relationships with colleagues from my work-life and found a little more time to exercise. I have continued to read many books (over 175 books since retirement).

I have been able to write three handbooks for advisors and hope to complete one or two more for advisors plus a book for clients of the financial advice industry.

When I retired, I thought I was only going to write one book for advisors but soon realized that several separate handbooks covering major topics would be more readable and, frankly, less overwhelming to write. I wrote this book first because I needed to record the processes for retirement and transitioning immediately while it was fresh in my mind.

While writing this book, I realized the need for the team-building handbook to be ready simultaneously, because how I managed my team facilitated my approach to transitioning my clientele upon retirement. Writing the "Seeking Group Referrals from Another Advisor" and "Transitioning Your Clientele to Your Successor" sections of this book revealed the need for a tool to help advisors easily articulate their unique business model, so I decided to develop the checklist tool for business model articulation to be readily accessible on my website. I then decided to write a book that describes and discusses the many potential components of advisors' business models for advisors of all ages and other industry participants. I decided that all three handbooks should be published simultaneously because they are so interrelated.

There are still not enough hours in the day. However, I am spending my retirement doing what I want to do and am enjoying it to the fullest. I hope the ideas and tools presented in this book will help many advisors do the same.

Afterword: COVID-19

With great crises come great opportunities

As I began the process of publishing the first three handbooks of this series, the world and the financial advice industry were suddenly facing the COVID-19 world pandemic health crisis. In addition to healthcare workers and people infected by the virus, the crisis dramatically affected the everyday lives and financial circumstances of a huge number of people in the world as countries closed their borders, schools, stores and restaurants, maintaining only essential services. Arts, sporting and social events around the world were canceled, and large populations were confined to their homes. Individuals, including advisors and clients, faced major challenges relating to childcare and eldercare. Economic activity ground to a halt; unemployment soared to historic levels; stock markets plummeted, and many businesses struggled to survive government mandated closures. The businesses that survived had to adapt to a new world of "social distancing". While living through this crisis, I reviewed the topics discussed in this handbook with the effects of the crisis in mind.

Part 1. Seeking Group Referrals from Another Advisor

Potential successors may have lost the opportunity to mingle in person with potentially retiring advisors during COVID-19, however they may have gained the opportunity to mingle with more advisors by participating in virtual branch meetings, seminars, etc. The crisis has drawn attention to the difficulties some senior advisors have with adoption of technology, especially when they are physically separated from their assistants. An advisor could volunteer to help a struggling senior advisor embrace and utilize technology to communicate with clients and team members remotely. This offer of assistance might allow the advisor to reveal competencies and compatibilities that the retiring advisor will be looking for in a potential successor.

More group referral opportunities may arise as some older advisors are uncomfortable adapting to the new "post-COVID-19" world, thereby convincing them to accelerate retirement plans. Advisors should also consider looking outside their firm for retiring advisors seeking a successor whose firm's infrastructure is more capable of providing the support needed in the changing environment.

Part 2. Transitioning Your Clientele to Your Successor

The choice of successor remains the most crucial aspect of the transition. The right successor inspires confidence during a crisis. Clients who are comfortable with the advisor and all aspects of their business model (especially communication, approach to investments, financial planning and costs) are much more likely to trust the successor's advice. The crisis confirmed the need to choose a successor who can adapt to changing circumstances. Retiring advisors can now ask potential successors how they adapted to the COVID-19 crisis. The successor's location in relation to clients may become less important if clients have already adapted to virtual appointments. The importance of a successor advisor's own financial stability becomes more evident during a crisis. It is very difficult to focus on clients when you are facing financial ruin yourself.

The COVID-19 crisis confirmed the effectiveness and fairness of the variable price contract for referral compensation. The variable price contract for the group referral of my clientele to my successors took some of the pressure off my successors because their ongoing payments were based on current revenue, and because their number of payments (total price) would be reduced if the markets (on which their fee-based revenue is based) did not recover for a long time. Crises and bear markets are stressful enough without the added pressure of unforgiving fixed referral payments. At the beginning of the crisis, with stock markets down 30% and looking like they might fall further, I mentioned to one of my successors that he might not have to pay me after the second valuation date if the markets don't recover in time. He said he would rather meet the targets and have to pay me. The variable contract gave my successors peace of mind, knowing that they could survive the crisis even if the markets suffered a huge long-term blow. Clearly, this was a good "win-win" contract.

Due to social distancing issues caused by COVID-19, successors may have to compensate for an inability to conduct physical meetings while integrating a referred clientele into their practice and during the period of overlapping service with the retiring advisor. Virtual face-to-face meetings are likely the best alternative to physical meetings. Clients, who may have refused virtual meetings in the past, may now be more comfortable with on camera meetings after having been introduced to virtual meetings by family members during the isolation period of the crisis. When social distancing rules are relaxed, there may still be a reluctance to meet in downtown offices making house visits and virtual meetings more popular.

A crisis is an opportunity for successor advisors to solidify relationships with newly transitioned clients. Clients will usually remember how their advisor made them feel during a crisis.

Part 3. The Retirement Exit Decision

The COVID-19 crisis experience may have shone a spotlight on issues mentioned in "Hints That It May Be Time to Start Preparing for Retirement" and "The Dangers of Waiting Too Long to Retire". Some senior advisor's personal experiences and new thoughts toward the future triggered by the crisis might inspire them to start preparing for retirement sooner than they expected.

I determined during the financial crisis of 2008 that I did not want to endure the stress of another bear market as an investment advisor. I am very relieved that I don't have to deal with an advisor's day-to-day stress and necessary actions of this crisis.

COVID-19 forced many advisors to work from home with initial limited access to their assistants whom they may have been relying on to compensate for the advisor's lack of familiarity with technology. Many of these advisors happily discovered the benefits of virtual meetings, etc. and will be more comfortable with the technology going forward. Advisors who continue to be overwhelmed and unwilling to embrace the changes in the use of technology brought about by COVID-19 should likely consider retirement.

— — —

A crisis like COVID-19 can be an extremely destructive and disruptive force throughout the world. As financial advisors, it is our job to minimize the impact of crises on our clients and to search out opportunities to serve clients better. Doing so will result in win-win scenarios where our clients benefit, and we continue to prove the value of the financial advice industry to society.

Appendix: Articulate Your Business Model

A comparison of the retiring and potential successor advisor practices' written business models should help the retiring advisor choose the right successor. I will describe the first step in articulating your business model and describe and show the checklist process I have created to help advisors quickly document their own unique business model.

First Step: Determine Overall Mission and Commitment to Clients

The first step in articulating your unique business model is articulating your overall mission and commitment to your clients. Your business model describes your clientele and shows how you achieve your commitment by describing your practice's services, products, processes, etc. right down to the selection of each potential service, investment, etc.

An Example: My Mission and Commitment to Clients

Very early in my career, I determined that my mission was to help clients achieve financial peace of mind. After reading the 100+ comments I received from my clients when I retired, I could see that my clients clearly appreciated the financial peace of mind that my team and I brought to them through our services and commitment to communication. The client comments ultimately reflected our unwritten commitment to our clients. I decided it was time (after 33 years in the business), to write down "our commitment to our clients."

Our commitment to our clients:

- We are committed to helping each of our clients achieve Financial Peace of Mind.

- We learn what Financial Peace of Mind means to each individual client.

- We employ a straightforward, easy to understand, disciplined approach to investing, designed to make it easier for clients to be patient in good times and bad.

- We work hard to present financial information and plans in easy to understand formats.

- We are very accessible to our clients. No question is a silly question.

- We don't want blind faith; we want our clients to understand the logic behind our advice and easily see for themselves that we are following through on our commitment to them.

I believe my prospecting and marketing efforts would have benefited by the above written articulation of this commitment. Eventually, my entire business model flowed from and contributed to our ultimate mission of each client's financial peace of mind.

A Checklist Process to Develop and/or Articulate an Advisor's Unique Business Model

To enable advisors to articulate and share their unique business model with minimal cost and effort, my website offers a downloadable, customizable checklist process to help advisors quickly identify most, if not all, aspects of their business model. They allow an advisor to add their own items and details to my ready-made lists. This appendix shows all of the checklists in the form of a fully completed sample including the resulting summary. The sample, also downloadable from my website, is based on the final year of my practice. I have also included a sample of a variation of the client communication service model checklist for advisors who segment their clientele into A, B, C, D clients. All of these checklists are explained and discussed in further detail in my handbook *Business Models for Financial Advisors* as we proceed through the checklists for the various business model components.

Business Model Checklists

Component 1: Identify Compatible/Sustainable Groups of Clients and Potential Clients

Identify Compatible Groups of Clients and Potential Clients

Professions/Occupations

x	business executives
x	lawyers
x	accountants
	doctors
	dentists
	pilots
	teachers/professors
	real estate agents
2 or 3	architects
< 10	engineers
	sports professionals
	trade: _____

Business Owners and Organizations

x	any type of small business
	businesses supplying/making products you like: _____
	businesses providing services that interest you: _____
	businesses relating to your hobbies: _____
	businesses in your neighborhood: _____
	entrepreneurs
x	charitable foundations
x	proprietorships
x	medical professional corporations
x	trusts
x	holding companies

Background/Social Groups

	advisor's ethnic background: _____
	familiar ethnic backgrounds: _____

Background/Social Groups (continued)

	minority language: _____
	shared life experience (immigrant, war veteran, etc.)
x	small town
x	big city
	previous career peers
	clients from previous career

Common Beliefs

	specific religious groups: _____
	political outlook: _____
	charitable causes: _____
	activist causes: _____

Common Interests

x	sports: __tennis__
x	vacation property: __cottage__
	fashion: _____
	art: _____
	theatre: _____
	music: _____
	use of social media: _____

Age Group

	teenager
	young adults
x	middle age
x	approaching retirement
>30%	early retirement
>20%	RRIF age 72+

Family Experiences

x	single
x	married
	divorced
x	widowed
x	big family
x	small family (only child)

Family Experiences (continued)

x	caring for children
x	caring for the elderly
	caring for a disabled person

Gender

x	women
	men
	gay women
	gay men
	transgender

Identify Criteria for Sustainable Individual Relationships

Personality Traits

x	introvert
	extrovert
x	optimist
	cynical
x	humble/modest
x	confident
x	collaborative
x	appreciates long-term relationships
x	delegator
x	thankful
x	patient
	sense of humour
	ambitious
	high risk taker
x	moderate risk taker
x	conservative
x	ultra-conservative
	short-term focus
x	long-term focus

Client Goals

x	protect family from loss of life/income
x	financial independence
x	retire comfortably
x	liquidity/access to capital
x	leave a legacy (heirs or charity)
	quick gains expected range of returns: _____
x	long-term gains expected range of returns: _6% - 10%_
x	fixed inc. expected return: _current 5yr GIC/gov't bond rates_
x	save for personal use real estate properties
x	maintain personal use real estate properties
	build rental real estate portfolio
x	plan for event (wedding or religious event)
x	spending/distributing wealth during lifetime
x	charitable giving during lifetime
x	train/teach their children
x	minimize tax
x	protect small business (personnel loss, marriage breakdown)
	small business succession planning

Client Service Requirements: Communication

x	accessible by phone
x	voicemail: _live person answers during office hours_
x	accessible by e-mail
	after business hours access to advisor
x	review meeting, advisor's office frequency: _annual_
x	review meeting, client's home/office frequency: _occasional_
x	out-of-town review meetings: _North Ontario town_
	virtual (screensharing) review frequency: _____
	virtual (camera) review meeting frequency: _____
x	minimum contact frequency: _annually_
x	maximum contact frequency: _weekly_
x	save/minimize client time requirements
	seminars and educational events
	invitations to entertainment events
x	written registered plan contribution reminders: _mail/e-mail_
x	call for registered plan contribution reminders

Client Service Requirements: Investing

x	looking for help with investment strategy and selection
	looking for help implementing predetermined strategy
	desire for someone to bounce stock pick ideas off
	desire to choose and hold their own investment ideas
	wants to be involved in selection of specific investments
	desire to time the markets
	desire for the latest, newest investment product
	desire sophisticated investment ideas (derivatives, etc.)
	interested in complex details of recommendations
x	prefer simplified description of recommendations
x	ability to be patient with volatile markets
x	online monthly/quarterly statements
x	customized package of tax slips, etc. for investments

Client Service Requirements: Financial Planning

x	prepare financial plan
x	financial plan year by year forecasting
	budgeting assistance
x	help in setting reasonable short- and long-term goals
x	retirement planning
x	protection planning (insurance)
x	estate planning
x	communicate with estate lawyer
x	charitable giving
x	financial planning for small business
	disabled person strategies

Client Service Requirements: Tax

	tax return preparation services
x	communicate with tax accountants
x	advice on tax strategies

Client's Comfort/Preference Re Payment for Advice & Service

x	appreciate the benefits of the advice and services offered
x	comfort with transaction commissions
x	comfort with fees based on asset values
	comfort with hourly rate
	comfort with flat fee for service (e.g. X$ per financial plan)
x	comfort with fees embedded in products (funds, GICs, etc.)
x	will the client benefit enough to justify the costs of advice

Profitability: Immediate and Potential

x	household annual revenue from client exceeds: _$2,000_
x	household investable assets exceed: _$500,000_
	client's current income exceeds: _____
	income growth potential
	potential inheritance
	source of quality referrals
x	member of profitable household

Component 2: The Service Component of a Financial Advisor's Business Model

Client Communication Service Model

Client Contact Methods	Service Performer		Frequency
	You and Your Team	Outsource	
personal phone calls with updates	x		as needed
personal phone calls re transactions	x		as needed
voicemail for incoming calls	x		after hours
personal e-mail	x		as needed
face-to-face review at advisor's office	x		annually
face-to-face review at client's location	x		as needed
online review	x		as needed
mailout/e-mail review	x		as needed
market update letters/e-mails	mass blast		quarterly
money manager update letters/e-mails	specific group		as needed
stock update letters/e-mails	specific group		as needed
newsletters			
host seminars			
client focus groups			
website postings			
blogs			
videos			
podcasts			
social media			

Client Reminders	Service Performer		Frequency
	You and Your Team	Outsource	
maturing GICs, CSBs, bonds, etc.	x		as needed
RRSP contributions	x		annually
TFSA contributions	x		annually
RESP contributions	x		annually
life insurance premium reminders	x		annually
disability insurance premium reminders	x		annually
critical illness premium reminders	x		annually
RRSP conversion to RRIF/annuity	x		annually
LIRA conversion to LRIF/annuity	x		annually
tax loss selling	x		annually

	Service Performer		
	You and		
Personal Touches	Your Team	Outsource	Frequency
holiday season cards	every client		annually
team picture	every client	photos	annually
family picture	10 clients		annually
holiday season gifts/donations	some clients	x	annually
sympathy cards/gifts	x		as needed
personal celebration gifts	rarely		special events
birthday cards/letters			
birthday calls			
sports/entertainment tickets	rarely		special events
individual client lunches/dinners	rarely		special events
individual client entertainment events	rarely		special events
book gifts	x		sometimes
referral thank-you calls	x		all referrals
referral thank-you gifts	x		sometimes

Investing Advice Service Model

	Service Performer		
	You and		
Overall Investment Advice Services	Your Team	Outsource	Discretionary
determine client's investment goals	x		x
educate: various strategies, securities, etc.	seminar		
educate: expectation of returns & volatility	seminar		
assess client risk tolerance	x		
summarize client financial position/details	x		
make asset class allocation decisions	flow chart		x
provide investment policy statement	x		x
implement (buy/sell investments)	x		x
consider tax effects of recommendations	x	consult acct	
year-end tax loss selling	x	consult acct	

Asset Class Exposure Security Sets

	Service Performer		
	You and		
Cash & Equivalents Exposure	Your Team	Outsource	Discretionary
high interest savings accounts	x		x
T-bills	x		x
firms' cash management accounts	x		x
money market funds			
bank paper (banker's acceptance)			
commercial paper			

Fixed Income Exposure

	Service Performer		
	You and Your Team	Outsource	Discretionary
GICs	X		X
gov't bonds: federal	X		X
gov't bonds: provincial	X		X
gov't bonds: municipal			
short-term (one to five years)	X		X
mid-term (six to ten years)			
long-term (over ten years)			
compounding bonds/strips	X		X
corporate bonds			
convertible bonds			
U.S. bonds	X		X
international bonds			
preferred shares	X		X
insured annuities	X	X	
mortgage-backed securities			
private mortgages			

Common Equities Exposure

	Service Performer		
	You and Your Team	Outsource	Discretionary
common stocks	X		X
all-cap	X		X
large-cap	X		X
mid-cap			
small-cap			
specific sector: _____			
Canadian	X		X
U.S.	X		X
international	X		X
emerging markets			
specific country/region: _____			

Alternatives Exposure

	Service Performer		
	You and Your Team	Outsource	Discretionary
commercial real estate	X		X
residential rental real estate			
commodities: _____			
foreign currencies: _____			

Alternatives Exposure (continued)

	Service Performer		
	You and Your Team	Outsource	Discretionary
cryptocurrencies: _____			
start-up companies			
private equities			

Investment Strategies

	Service Performer		
	You and Your Team	Outsource	Discretionary
passive maturity ladder	x		x
passive fixed income (indexes)			
monthly income			
high-yield fixed income			
interest rate speculation			
passive equity (indexes)			
equity top-down by sector			
equity top-down by country			
equity bottom-up all sectors	x		x
equity bottom-up all countries	x		x
equity style growth	x		x
equity style value	x		x
equity style momentum			
equity style core			
equity style GARP	x		x
equity style high dividend			
socially responsible investing			
sustainable or ESG investing			
dollar cost averaging	x		
pre-authorized contributions	x		
rebalancing	x		x
covered call equity strategy			
borrowing to invest			
options strategy: _____			
currency hedging			
currency speculation			
selling short: _____			

Investment Delivery Vehicles	Service Performer		
	You and Your Team	Outsource	Discretionary
individual high interest savings accounts	x		x
individual t-bills	x		
money market funds			
commercial paper			
individual bonds: _fed and prov gov't_	x		x
individual GICs: _CDIC insured_	x		x
individual preferred shares: _big banks_	≥p2		
individual common stocks: _____			
initial public offerings: _preferreds_	x		x
ETFs bond indexes			
ETFs balanced indexes			
ETFs stock indexes			
ETFs managed			
ETFs: _____			
mutual funds bonds			
mutual funds balanced			
mutual funds stocks	x		x
mutual funds alternatives			
SMA* fixed income portfolios			
SMA* balanced portfolios			
SMA* equity portfolios	x	firm	x
SMA*: _____			
pools			
seg./guaranteed investment funds			
universal life			
insured annuities personal	x	firm	
insured annuities corporate	x	firm	
options, derivatives			
structured products (linked notes)			
futures			
hedge funds			
private equity			
limited partnerships: _____			
income trusts (including REITS)	x		x
tax assisted investments			
real estate property direct ownership			

* SMA = Separately Managed Accounts

Investment Platforms

	Service Performer		
	You and Your Team	Outsource	Discretionary
transaction commissions	x		
fee-based	x		x
separately managed accounts (third party)		firm	x
advisor managed accounts (discretionary)	x		x

Investment Account Types

	Service Performer		
	You and Your Team	Outsource	Discretionary
investment accounts	x	firm	x
investment margin accounts	x	firm	x
third party custodial accounts			
combined investment & banking accounts	x	firm	x
delivery against payment (DAP, DVP)			
receive against payment (RAP, RVP)			
universal life policies	x	external	
Tax-Free Savings Account (TFSA)	x	firm	x
Registered Disability Savings Plan (RDSP)			
Registered Education Savings Plan (RESP)	x	firm	x
Registered Retirement Savings Plan (RRSP)	x	firm	x
Locked-In Retirement Account (LIRA)	x	firm	x
Locked-In Retirement Savings Plan (LRSP)	x	firm	x
Individual Pension Plan (IPP)	x	firm	x
Registered Retirement Income Fund (RRIF)	x	firm	x
Restricted Life Income Fund (RLIF)	x	firm	x
Locked-In Retirement Income Fund (LRIF)	x	firm	x
Life Income Fund (LIF)	x	firm	x
Life annuities	x	external	
donor-advised charitable giving accounts	x	firm	x
multiple currency: _US_EURO_AUS_UK_	x	firm	x

Investment Reporting

	Service Performer		
	You and Your Team	Outsource	Frequency
mandatory statements		firm	4 to 12
online statements		firm	4 to 12
custom portfolio summary	x		1 to 12
performance: minimum required		firm	annually
performance: special reports	x	firm	on demand

Tax Reporting for Investments	Service Performer		
	You and Your Team	Outsource	Frequency
mandatory year-end tax package		firm	annually
personalized client tax document checklist	70%		
custom year-end tax package to client	50%		annually
custom annual tax package to accountant	10%		annually
custom compound bond interest summary	x		annually
YTD capital gain/loss reports	x	firm	as needed
unrealized gain/loss reports	x	firm	as needed

Financial Planning Service Model

Overall Financial Planning Services	Service Performer		
	You and Your Team	Outsource	Frequency
set realistic financial goals	x		annually
year by year forecasts	x		annually
budgeting	x		annually
event expense planning	x		annually
retirement planning and advice	x		annually
pension advice	x		annually
retirement income & cash flow decisions	x		annually
protection: legal documents	x		annually
protection: insurance	x		annually
estate planning	x		annually
special situations	x	external	annually
small business	x	external	annually
disabled person strategies		both	annually

Steps: Provide Financial Planning Services	Service Performer		
	You and Your Team	Outsource	Frequency
information gathering	x		annually
setting and confirming goals	x		annually
info input into FP software	x		annually
analysis of forecasts and needs	x		annually
prepare recommendations	x		annually
presentation to client	x		annually
multiple scenarios	x		annually

| | Service Performer | | |
| | You and | | |
Set Realistic Financial Goals	Your Team	Outsource	Frequency
annual income - working years	x		as needed
lifestyle spending - working years	x		as needed
annual savings - working years	x		as needed
annual income - retirement years	x		as needed
lifestyle spending - retirement years	x		as needed
annual savings - retirement years	x		as needed
debt repayment targets	x		as needed
spending on major events/purchases	x		as needed
return on investments	x		as needed
minimize income taxes payable	x		as needed
minimize estate taxes payable	x		as needed
liquid assets value at specific time	x		as needed
net worth at specific time	x		as needed
estate value for heirs	x		as needed
real estate value	x		as needed

| | Service Performer | | |
| | You and | | |
Year By Year Forecasts	Your Team	Outsource	Frequency
forecast by individual	x		as needed
forecast by household	x		as needed
forecasts include companies	x		as needed
lifestyle spending	x		always
annual savings non-registered	x		as needed
annual savings TFSA	x		as needed
annual savings RRSP	x		as needed
annual savings RESP	x		as needed
sources of external cash flow	x		always
government income (CPP, OAS)	x		always
sources of self-financed cash flow	x		always
income taxes payable	x		as needed
OAS clawback	x		as needed
liquid assets value (total)	x		always
liquid assets value by acct type	x		always
investment asset class allocations	x		always
expected return (changing risk tolerance)	x		always
life insurance cash surrender value	x		as needed
outstanding debts	x		as needed
real estate value	x		as needed
net worth	x		always

Year By Year Forecasts (continued)

	Service Performer		
	You and Your Team	Outsource	Frequency
costs of final arrangements (funeral, etc.)			
estate taxes (cap gains, RRSP/RRIF, etc.)	x		as needed
probate fees	x		always
estate after-tax value	x		as needed
graphs	x		as needed

Budgeting

	Service Performer		
	You and Your Team	Outsource	Frequency
provide budget template			
estimate annual spending	x		as needed
plan for saving	x		as needed
plan for tax installments	x		as needed
plan for charitable giving	x		as needed
provide expense analysis			
provide debt analysis	x		as needed
provide mortgage review	x		as needed
provide budget review			

Event Expense Planning

	Service Performer		
	You and Your Team	Outsource	Frequency
home purchase or sale	x		as needed
vacation property purchase/sale	x		as needed
large item purchase (car, etc.)	x		as needed
education	x		as needed
religious event	x		as needed
special trip	x		as needed
wedding	x		as needed
divorce			

Retirement Planning

Pre-Retirement Analysis and Advice

	Service Performer		
	You and Your Team	Outsource	Frequency
retirement goals	x		annually
retirement financial needs	x		annually
retirement income	x		annually
savings strategies (how much, when)	x		annually

Pre-Retirement Analysis and Advice (continued)

	Service Performer		
	You and Your Team	Outsource	Frequency
savings allocation decisions (account type)	x		ongoing
use of registered accts (TFSAs, RRSPs, etc.)	x		ongoing
designate beneficiary/successor annuitant	x		as needed
potential loss of employer benefits			
evaluation early retirement package	x		as needed

Pension Advice

	Service Performer		
	You and Your Team	Outsource	Frequency
group pension plans (investments, etc.)	x		as needed
pension plan choices (investments, etc.)	x		as needed
IPPs (independent pension plans)	x		rare
compare: pension, locked-in RRSP, annuity	x		as needed
risk analysis of corp. pension (funding, etc.)	x		rare
risk analysis of senior exec retirement plan	x		rare
spousal survivor pension benefits	x		as needed

Retirement Income & Cash Flow Decisions

	Service Performer		
	You and Your Team	Outsource	Frequency
OAS timing decision	x		as needed
CPP timing decision	x		as needed
CPP income splitting	x		as needed
company pension benefit start date	x		as needed
company pension income splitting	x		as needed
timing of RRSP conversion to RRIF	x		as needed
RRIF/LIF, etc. withdrawal decisions	x		as needed
RRIF/LIF, etc. vs annuity decisions	x		as needed
unlocking LIF/LRIF pension plans	x		as needed
deregistering RRSP/RRIF	x		as needed

Protection

Legal Documents

	Service Performer		
	You and Your Team	Outsource	Frequency
provide names of lawyers to draft POA(s)	x		on request
consider suitable POA attorney(s)	x		as needed
consider institutional POA attorney	x		as needed
assist preparation prior to drafting POAs	x		as needed

Legal Documents (continued)

| | Service Performer | | |
	You and Your Team	Outsource	Frequency
draft POA personal care		external	as needed
draft POA financial		external	as needed
review POA(s) personal care			
review POA(s) financial			
prenup or cohab agreement			
postnup agreement			
trusts for married adult children			

Insurance

| | Service Performer | | |
	You and Your Team	Outsource	Frequency
life insurance needs analysis	x	firm	as needed
term life	x	firm	as needed
whole life (permanent)	x	firm	as needed
disability	x	firm	as needed
critical illness	x	firm	as needed
long-term care			
extended health care			
property: home or tenant			
auto			

Estate Planning

Preparation Prior to Drafting of Wills

| | Service Performer | | |
	You and Your Team	Outsource	Frequency
assess need to update will	annually		
review existing will		x	
provide names of lawyers to draft will(s)	as needed		
list of all financial assets/obligations	as needed		
list of insurance policies with details	as needed		
provide questionnaire of personal info.	as needed		
prepare list of personal assets (art, etc.)			
prepare list of digital assets			

Identify Issues to Raise with Lawyer

| | Service Performer | | |
	You and Your Team	Outsource	Frequency
consider suitable executors/trustees	x		
consider institutional executor/trustee	as needed		
consider executor/trustee fees	x		

Identify Issues to Raise with Lawyer (continued)	Service Performer		
	You and Your Team	Outsource	Frequency
probate taxes	x		
Cdn. taxes at death (cap gains, RRSPs, etc.)	x		
U.S. taxes at death (real estate, securities)	x		
international taxes at death (real estate)			
life insurance (whole or universal life)	x	firm	
vacation property transition strategies	x		
legal obligations (alimony, child support)			
heirs capability of handling inheritance	x		
potential need for testamentary trusts	x		
maximize wealth transfer	x	firm	
small business transition			
Corporate Estate Bond	x	firm	
charitable giving	x		
digital assets			
subscriber rights for RESPs	x		
maintain investment advisor relationship	x		

Drafting of Wills	Service Performer		
	You and Your Team	Outsource	Frequency
attend will preparation meetings	on request		on request
draft primary will		external	
draft secondary will(s) (business, intl, etc.)		external	
review will(s)	on request	x	

Special Situations	Service Performer		
	You and Your Team	Outsource	Frequency
severance issues	x		as needed
divorce			
death in family	x		as needed
severe illness in family	x		as needed
client named as POA	x		as needed
client named as executor	x		as needed

Small Business

	Service Performer		
	You and Your Team	Outsource	Frequency
key person insurance			
protect from marriage breakdown			
succession (unexpected event)			
succession for retirement			
income smoothing	x	external	as needed
corporate estate bond	x	external	as needed

Disabled Person Strategies

	Service Performer		
	You and Your Team	Outsource	Frequency
Registered Disability Savings Plan			
lifetime benefit trusts			
qualifying trust annuities			
qualified disability trusts			
Henson trusts			
gov't disability support programs			
income tax credits			
RESP ramifications			

Tax Return and Tax Strategies Service Model

Tax Return Services

	Service Performer		
	You and Your Team	Outsource	Frequency
see Tax Reporting for Investing checklist	x		
prepare year-end tax returns			
answer accountant's questions	x		as needed
access to trusted tax experts		x	as needed
referral list: trusted tax accountants	x		as needed

Tax Strategies

	Service Performer		
	You and Your Team	Outsource	Frequency
consult accountants: proposed action effect	x	x	as needed
timing of gains and losses	x	external	as needed
tax loss selling	x	external	annually
income splitting strategies	x	external	
timing and allocation of reg. acct. contrib	x	external	

| | Service Performer | | |
| | You and | | |
Tax Strategies (continued)	Your Team	Outsource	Frequency
spousal loan for income splitting	x	external	as needed
income and expense timing	x	external	
charitable giving: in-kind donations	x	external	as needed
donor advised charitable foundations	x	external	as needed
holding companies special considerations		external	
trusts special considerations		external	
family trusts		external	
estate freezes		external	
farm properties		external	

Component 3: Processes and Presentations

There is no checklist for this component. However, I intend to dedicate an entire future handbook to the subject.

Component 4: Determine Needed Resources and Suppliers/Sources

Software Programs and Tech Tools	Need	Source		
		Available from Firm	Advisor Paid Created or Modified	External Supplier
contact management	x	x	x	Goldmine
tax reporting	x	x	x	
portfolio reporting	x	x	x	
performance reporting	x	x		
financial planning program (in depth)	x	FP Solution	x	
financial planning program (quick)		Razor		
every day templates, macros, etc.	x	x	x	
monthly/quarterly statements	x	x		
practice evaluation reports	x	x	x	

Team	Need	Source		
		Available from Firm	Advisor Paid Created or Modified	External Supplier
team member salaries	x	3	3.5	
team member bonuses	x	0	6.5	
team appreciation events	x	x	x	
gifts to team members	x		x	

Training/Education:Advisor & Team	Need	Source		
		Available from Firm	Advisor Paid Created or Modified	External Supplier
software	x	x	x	x
marketing	x	x	x	x
practice management	x	x	x	x
client communication	x	x	x	x
investing	x	x	x	x
financial planning	x	x	x	x
tax	x	x	x	x

Client Education	Need	Source		
		Available from Firm	Advisor Paid Created or Modified	External Supplier
mutual fund reports	x	x	x	x
separately managed acct reports	x	x	x	x
common stock reports		x		x
market history reports	x	x	x	x
RRSP, RRIF, TFSA, RESP info	x	x		x
life insurance strategy info	x	x	x	x
income replacement info	x	x		x
estate planning strategy info	x	x		x
POA, executor, trustee info	x	x		x
tax strategy reports	x	x		x
government budget reports	x	x		x

Marketing	Need	Source		
		Available from Firm	Advisor Paid Created or Modified	External Supplier
website builder	x	x	x	
newsletter builder		x		
newsletter content		x	x	mny mgrs
brochures online	x	x	x	
brochures printed		partial	x	
client appreciation events	rare	partial	very rare	
client gifts	x		x	
Andex Charts	x			fund cos

Investment Research	Need	Source		
		Available from Firm	Advisor Paid Created or Modified	External Supplier
mutual fund analysis	x	x		x
money manager due diligence	x	x	x	x
common stocks (in-house)	rare	x		
preferred shares (in-house)	x	x		
corporate bonds (in-house)		x		
in-house screening program: _____				
client online access to research	x	x		
client online screening of research				
Bloomberg	x	x		

Investment Research (continued)

	Need	Source		
		Available from Firm	Advisor Paid Created or Modified	External Supplier
external screening program: _CPMS_				
external source: _ Credit Suisse_	rare	x		
external source: _ Value Line_	rare	x		

Specialists

	Need	Source		
		Available from Firm	Advisor Paid Created or Modified	External Supplier
insurance	x	x		
financial planner		x		
trust and estate planning	x	x		x
legal	x	x		x
tax	x	x		x

Office

	Need	Source		
		Available from Firm	Advisor Paid Created or Modified	External Supplier
real estate: _location, space_	x	x		
advisor private office	x			
home office	x		x	
remote access: _advisor & team_	x	x	x	
computer hardware	x	x		
furnishings	x	x	x	
printers, fax, scanners, etc.	x	partial	partial	
office materials	x	partial	partial	
mail services	x	x		
courier services	x		x	

Component 5: Pricing and Client Costs Model

Direct Charges

Commission/Transaction/Trading Charges

	Incurred	Frequency
purchase of bond _0.2%/yr, max 1%_	x	at execution
sale of bond _0 - 0.2%/yr, max 1%_	x	at execution
purchase of preferred share _0.2%/yr, max 1%_	x	at execution
sale of preferred share _0.2%/yr, max 1%_	x	at execution
buy common stock _min $140 , max 1% (unsol)_	occasional	at execution
sale common stock _min $140, max 1% (unsol)_	occasional	at execution
options _____		
futures _____		
mutual fund front end _____		
commission: _____		
commission: _____		
commission: _____		
mutual fund switch or change fees: _____		
mutual fund redemption fees	rare	at execution

Advisor Annual Fee % Based on Client Assets

	Incurred	Frequency
% based on total of all assets managed: _____		
cash: _0.0%_	x	quarterly
gov't guaranteed bonds/GICs: _0.2%_	x	quarterly
preferred shares: _0.2% big bank rate reset_	x	quarterly
common stock picking: _____		
equity mutual funds: _1.0% F-series_	x	quarterly
balanced mutual funds: _____		
fixed income mutual funds: _____		
separately managed equity: _1.5% - 2.25%_	x	quarterly
separately managed fixed income: _____		
minimum annual: _$2,000 ($0 advisor managed)_	x	quarterly

Fee Only (hourly, annual or fee-for-service)

	Incurred	Frequency
hourly rate: $_(range)_		
flat charge for year: $_____		
preparation of initial financial plan: $_(range)_		
update of financial plan: $_(range)_		

Fee Based on Performance

% based on return: _(description)_

Incurred	Frequency

Administration/Operating Charges

admin fee (RRSP, RRIF, LIF, etc.): _$125_

TFSA fee: _$75 ($0:fee-based/assets >$100,000)_

RESP fee: _$75 ($0:fee-based/assets >$100,000)_

small household fee: _($125-$250)_

inactivity fee: _____

special account fee: _$200 ($0 if fee-based)_

transfer out fee: _$100_

banking fee (wiring, etc.)

safekeeping fees (paper certificates): _____

interest charged on margin accounts: _____

custodial fees

admin fee: _____

Incurred	Frequency
x	annually
rare	annually
rare	annually
rare	annually
rare	annually
x	annually
x	on execution
rare	annually

Indirect Charges

trailing commissions (mutual funds, ETFs)

fees embedded in financial products (GICs, etc.)

fees embedded in currency conversion

back-end fund purchase commission: _____

product fees (commission paid by supplier)

fund management fees

mutual fund MERs: _1.0% - 1.35%_

mutual fund trading fees (TER)

new issue commissions paid by issuer

fees embedded in life annuity products

fees embedded in life insurance products

referral fees: _advisor pays for receiving referral_

finders fees: _advisor paid for finding a mortgage_

Incurred	Frequency
x	monthly
x	on execution
rare	on execution
x	
x	
x	
x	on execution
x	on execution
x	on execution
rare	varies
rare	on execution

Resulting Summary of Business Model

C Timms Sample (Advisor Name)
Summary: Compatible Groups and Criteria for Sustainable Relationships
Date

IDENTIFY COMPATIBLE/TARGET GROUPS

Professions/Occupations

x	business executives
x	lawyers
x	accountants
2 or 3	architects
< 10	engineers

Business Owners and Organizations

x	any type of small business
x	charitable foundations
x	proprietorships
x	medical professional corporations
x	trusts
x	holding companies

Background/Social Groups

x	small town
x	big city

Common Interests

x	sports: _tennis_
x	vacation property: _cottage_

Age Group

x	middle age
x	approaching retirement
> 30%	early retirement
> 20%	RRIF age 72+

Family Experiences

x	single
x	married
x	widowed
x	big family
x	small family (only child)
x	caring for children
x	caring for the elderly

Gender

x	women

CRITERIA FOR SUSTAINABLE INDIVIDUAL RELATIONSHIPS

Personality Traits

x	introvert
x	optimist
x	humble/modest
x	confident
x	collaborative
x	appreciates long-term relationships
x	delegator
x	thankful
x	patient
x	moderate risk taker
x	conservative
x	ultra-conservative
x	long-term focus

Client Goals

x	protect family from loss of life/income
x	financial independence
x	retire comfortably
x	liquidity/access to capital
x	leave a legacy (heirs or charity)
x	long-term gains expected range of returns: _6% - 10%_
x	fixed inc. expected return: _current 5yr GIC/gov't bond rates_
x	save for personal use real estate properties
x	maintain personal use real estate properties

Client Goals (continued)

x	plan for event (wedding or religious event)
x	spending/distributing wealth during lifetime
x	charitable giving during lifetime
x	train/teach their children
x	minimize tax
x	protect small business (personnel loss, marriage breakdown)

Client Service Requirements: Communication

x	accessible by phone
x	voicemail: _live person answers during office hours_
x	accessible by e-mail
x	review meeting, advisor's office frequency: _annual_
x	review meeting, client's home/office frequency: _occasional_
x	out-of-town review meetings: _North Ontario town_
x	minimum contact frequency: _annually_
x	maximum contact frequency: _weekly_
x	save/minimize client time requirements
x	written registered plan contribution reminders: _mail/e-mail_
x	call for registered plan contribution reminders

Client Service Requirements: Investing

x	looking for help with investment strategy and selection
x	prefer simplified description of recommendations
x	ability to be patient with volatile markets
x	online monthly/quarterly statements
x	customized package of tax slips, etc. for investments

Client Service Requirements: Financial Planning

x	prepare financial plan
x	financial plan year by year forecasting
x	help in setting reasonable short- and long-term goals
x	retirement planning
x	protection planning (insurance)
x	estate planning
x	communicate with estate lawyer
x	charitable giving
x	financial planning for small business

Client Service Requirements: Tax

x
x

communicate with tax accountants

advice on tax strategies

Client's Comfort/Preference Re Payment for Advice & Service

x
x
x
x
x

appreciate the benefits of the advice and services offered

comfort with transaction commissions

comfort with fees based on asset values

comfort with fees embedded in products (funds, GICs, etc.)

will the client benefit enough to justify the costs of advice

Profitability: Immediate and Potential

x
x
x

household annual revenue from client exceeds:_$2,000_

household investable assets exceed:_$500,000_

member of profitable household

COMMENTS

I have converted 80% of my clients to fee-based, likely 10% more to do.

I have converted about 50% of clients to discretionary.

C Timms Sample (Advisor Name)
Summary Of Service Model for Client Communication
Date

Client Contact Methods	You and Your Team	Outsource	Frequency
personal phone calls with updates	x		as needed
personal phone calls re transactions	x		as needed
voicemail for incoming calls	x		after hours
personal e-mail	x		as needed
face-to-face review at advisor's office	x		annually
face-to-face review at client's location	x		as needed
online review	x		as needed
mailout/e-mail review	x		as needed
market update letters/e-mails	mass blast		quarterly
money manager update letters/e-mails	specific group		as needed
stock update letters/e-mails	specific group		as needed

The "Service Performer" header spans "You and Your Team" and "Outsource".

Client Reminders	You and Your Team	Outsource	Frequency
maturing GICs, CSBs, bonds, etc.	x		as needed
RRSP contributions	x		annually
TFSA contributions	x		annually
RESP contributions	x		annually
life insurance premium reminders	x		annually
disability insurance premium reminders	x		annually
critical illness premium reminders	x		annually
RRSP conversion to RRIF/annuity	x		annually
LIRA conversion to LRIF/annuity	x		annually
tax loss selling	x		annually

Personal Touches	You and Your Team	Outsource	Frequency
holiday season cards	every client		annually
team picture	every client	photos	annually
family picture	10 clients		annually
holiday season gifts/donations	some clients	x	annually
sympathy cards/gifts	x		as needed
personal celebration gifts	rarely		special events
sports/entertainment tickets	rarely		special events
individual client lunches/dinners	rarely		special events
individual client entertainment events	rarely		special events
book gifts	x		sometimes
referral thank-you calls	x		all referrals
referral thank-you gifts	x		sometimes

C Timms Sample (Advisor Name)
Summary of Service Model for Investing
Date

Overall Investment Advice Services	Service Performer		
	You and Your Team	Outsource	Discretionary
determine client's investment goals	x		x
educate: various strategies, securities, etc.	seminar		
educate: expectation of returns & volatility	seminar		
assess client risk tolerance	x		
summarize client financial position/details	x		
make asset class allocation decisions	flow chart		x
provide investment policy statement	x		x
implement (buy/sell investments)	x		x
consider tax effects of recommendations	x	accountant	
year-end tax loss selling	x	accountant	

Steps: Security Selection for Product Shelf

select asset class exposure security sets	x		x
select investment strategies	x		x
select investment delivery vehicles	x		x
choose securities for product shelf	x		

Asset Class Exposure Security Sets

Cash & Equivalents Exposure

high interest savings accounts	x		x
T-bills	x		x
firms' cash management accounts	x		x

Fixed Income Exposure

GICs	x		x
gov't bonds: federal	x		x
gov't bonds: provincial	x		x
short-term (one to five years)	x		x
compounding bonds/strips	x		x
U.S. bonds	x		x
preferred shares	x		x
insured annuities	x	x	

Common Equities Exposure

common stocks	X		X
all-cap	X		X
large-cap	X		X
Canadian	X		X
U.S.	X		X
international	X		X

Alternatives Exposure

commercial real estate	X		X

Investment Strategies

passive maturity ladder	X		X
equity bottom-up all sectors	X		X
equity bottom-up all countries	X		X
equity style growth	X		X
equity style value	X		X
equity style GARP	X		X
dollar cost averaging	X		
pre-authorized contributions	X		
rebalancing	X		X

Investment Delivery Vehicles

individual high interest savings accounts	X		X
individual t-bills	X		
individual bonds: _fed and prov gov't_	X		X
individual GICs: _CDIC insured_	X		X
individual preferred shares: _big banks_	≥p2		
initial public offerings: _preferreds_	X		X
mutual funds stocks	X		X
SMA* equity portfolios	X	firm	X
insured annuities personal	X	firm	
insured annuities corporate	X	firm	
income trusts (including REITS)	X		X

Investment Platforms

transaction commissions	X		
fee-based	X		X
separately managed accounts (third party)		firm	X
advisor managed accounts (discretionary)	X		X

Investment Account Types

investment accounts	X	firm	X
investment margin accounts	X	firm	X
combined investment & banking accounts	X	firm	X
universal life policies	X	X	

Investment Account Types (continued)

Tax-Free Savings Account (TFSA)	x	firm	x
Registered Education Savings Plan (RESP)	x	firm	x
Registered Retirement Savings Plan (RRSP)	x	firm	x
Locked-In Retirement Account (LIRA)	x	firm	x
Locked-In Retirement Savings Plan (LRSP)	x	firm	x
Individual Pension Plan (IPP)	x	firm	x
Registered Retirement Income Fund (RRIF)	x	firm	x
Restricted Life Income Fund (RLIF)	x	firm	x
Locked-In Retirement Income Fund (LRIF)	x	firm	x
Life Income Fund (LIF)	x	firm	x
Life annuities	x	x	
donor-advised charitable giving accounts	x	firm	x
multiple currency: _US_EURO_AUS_UK_	x	firm	x

Investment Reporting

			Frequency
mandatory statements		firm	4 to 12
online statements		firm	4 to 12
custom portfolio summary	x		1 to 12
performance: minimum required		firm	annually
performance: special reports	x	firm	on demand

Tax Reporting for Investments

mandatory year-end tax package		firm	annually
personalized client tax document checklist	70%		
custom year-end tax package to client	50%		annually
custom annual tax package to accountant	10%		annually
custom compound bond interest summary	x		annually
YTD capital gain/loss reports	x	firm	as needed
unrealized gain/loss reports	x	firm	as needed

COMMENTS

Approximately 60% of clients have discretionary accounts, expect more as clients age.

C Timms Sample (Advisor Name)
Summary of Financial Planning Service Model
Date

Overall Financial Planning Services	Service Performer		
	You and Your Team	Outsource	Frequency
set realistic financial goals	x		annually
year by year forecasts	x		annually
budgeting	x		annually
event expense planning	x		annually
retirement planning and advice	x		annually
pension advice	x		annually
retirement income & cash flow decision	x		annually
protection: legal documents	x		annually
protection: insurance	x		annually
estate planning	x		annually
special situations	x	external	annually
small business	x	external	annually
disabled person strategies		both	annually

Steps: Provide Financial Planning Services			
information gathering	x		annually
setting and confirming goals	x		annually
info input into FP software	x		annually
analysis of forecasts and needs	x		annually
prepare recommendations	x		annually
presentation to client	x		annually
multiple scenarios	x		annually

Set Realistic Financial Goals			
annual income - working years	x		as needed
lifestyle spending - working years	x		as needed
annual savings - working years	x		as needed
annual income - retirement years	x		as needed
lifestyle spending - retirement years	x		as needed
annual savings - retirement years	x		as needed
debt repayment targets	x		as needed
spending on major events/purchases	x		as needed
return on investments	x		as needed
minimize income taxes payable	x		as needed
minimize estate taxes payable	x		as needed
liquid assets value at specific time	x		as needed

Set Realistic Financial Goals (continued)

net worth at specific time	x		as needed
estate value for heirs	x		as needed
real estate value	x		as needed

Year By Year Forecasts

forecast by individual	x		as needed
forecast by household	x		as needed
forecasts include companies	x		as needed
lifestyle spending	x		always
annual savings non-registered	x		as needed
annual savings TFSA	x		as needed
annual savings RRSP	x		as needed
annual savings RESP	x		as needed
sources of external cash flow	x		always
government income (CPP, OAS)	x		always
sources of self-financed cash flow	x		always
income taxes payable	x		as needed
OAS clawback	x		as needed
liquid assets value (total)	x		always
liquid assets value by acct type	x		always
investment asset class allocations	x		always
expected return (changing risk tolerance)	x		always
life insurance cash surrender value	x		as needed
outstanding debts	x		as needed
real estate value	x		as needed
net worth	x		always
estate taxes (cap gains, RRSP/RRIF, etc.)	x		as needed
probate fees	x		always
estate after-tax value	x		as needed
graphs	x		as needed

Budgeting

estimate annual spending	x		as needed
plan for saving	x		as needed
plan for tax installments	x		as needed
plan for charitable giving	x		as needed
provide debt analysis	x		as needed
provide mortgage review	x		as needed

Event Expense Planning

home purchase or sale	x		as needed
vacation property purchase/sale	x		as needed
large item purchase (car, etc.)	x		as needed

Event Expense Planning (continued)

education	x		as needed
religious event	x		as needed
special trip	x		as needed
wedding	x		as needed

Retirement Planning

Pre-Retirement Analysis and Advice

retirement goals	x		annually
retirement financial needs	x		annually
retirement income	x		annually
savings strategies (how much, when)	x		annually
savings allocation decisions (account type)	x		ongoing
use of registered accts (TFSAs, RRSPs, etc.)	x		ongoing
designate beneficiary/successor annuitant	x		as needed
evaluation early retirement package	x		as needed

Pension Advice

group pension plans (investments, etc.)	x		as needed
pension plan choices (investments, etc.)	x		as needed
IPPs (independent pension plans)	x		rare
compare: pension, locked-in RRSP, annuity	x		as needed
risk analysis of corp. pension (funding, etc.)	x		rare
risk analysis of senior exec retirement plan	x		rare
spousal survivor pension benefits	x		as needed

Retirement Income and Cash Flow Decisions

OAS timing decision	x		as needed
CPP timing decision	x		as needed
CPP income splitting	x		as needed
company pension benefit start date	x		as needed
company pension income splitting	x		as needed
timing of RRSP conversion to RRIF	x		as needed
RRIF/LIF, etc. withdrawal decisions	x		as needed
RRIF/LIF, etc. vs annuity decisions	x		as needed
unlocking LIF/LRIF pension plans	x		as needed
deregistering RRSP/RRIF	x		as needed

Protection

Legal Documents

provide names of lawyers to draft POA(s)	x		on request
consider suitable POA attorney(s)	x		as needed
consider institutional POA attorney	x		as needed
assist preparation prior to drafting POAs	x		as needed

Legal Documents (continued)

draft POA personal care		external	as needed
draft POA financial		external	as needed

Insurance

life insurance needs analysis	x	firm	as needed
term life	x	firm	as needed
whole life (permanent)	x	firm	as needed
disability	x	firm	as needed
critical illness	x	firm	as needed

Estate Planning

Preparation Prior to Drafting of Wills

assess need to update will	annually		
review existing will		on request	
provide names of lawyers to draft will(s)	as needed		
list of all financial assets/obligations	as needed		
list of insurance policies with details	as needed		
provide questionnaire of personal info.	as needed		

Identify Issues to Raise with Lawyer

consider suitable executors/trustees	x		
consider institutional executor/trustee	as needed		
consider executor/trustee fees	x		
probate taxes	x		
Cdn. taxes at death (cap gains, RRSPs, etc.)	x		
U.S. taxes at death (real estate, securities)	x		
life insurance (whole or universal life)	x	firm	
vacation property transition strategies	x		
heirs capability of handling inheritance	x		
potential need for testamentary trusts	x		
maximize wealth transfer	x	firm	
Corporate Estate Bond	x	firm	
charitable giving	x		
subscriber rights for RESPs	x		
maintain investment advisor relationship	x		

Drafting of Wills

attend will preparation meetings	on request		on request
draft primary will		external	
draft secondary will(s) (business, intl, etc.)		external	
review will(s)	on request	x	

Special Situations

severance issues	x		as needed
death in family	x		as needed
severe illness in family	x		as needed
client named as POA	x		as needed
client named as executor	x		as needed

Small Business

income smoothing	x	external	as needed
corporate estate bond	x	external	as needed

COMMENTS

We have completed financial plans for every client that was interested.

We usually updated the financial plan as part of the client's annual review.

C Timms Sample (Advisor Name)
Summary of Service Model for Tax Services
Date

Tax Return Services

	Service Performer		
	You and Your Team	**Outsource**	**Frequency**
see Tax Reporting for Investing checklist	x		
answer accountant's questions	x		as needed
access to trusted tax experts		x	as needed
referral list: trusted tax accountants	x		as needed

Tax Strategies

	You and Your Team	Outsource	Frequency
consult accountants: proposed action effect	x	x	as needed
timing of gains and losses	x	external	as needed
tax loss selling	x	external	annually
income splitting strategies	x	external	
timing and allocation of reg. acct. contrib	x	external	
spousal loan for income splitting	x	external	as needed
income and expense timing	x	external	
charitable giving: in-kind donations	x	external	as needed
donor advised charitable foundations	x	external	as needed
holding companies special considerations		external	
trusts special considerations		external	
family trusts		external	
estate freezes		external	
farm properties		external	

COMMENTS
I have no interest in preparing tax returns.
I do all I can to work with, assist and provide info to client's tax professionals.
I am always looking for tax strategies that may be appropriate for our clients.

C Timms Sample (Advisor Name)
Summary of Needed Resources and Potential Sources
Date

Software Programs and Tech Tools	Need	Source		
		Available from Firm	Advisor Paid Created or Modified	External Supplier
contact management	x	x	x	Goldmine
tax reporting	x	x	x	
portfolio reporting	x	x	x	
performance reporting	x	x		
financial planning program (in depth)	x	FP Solution	x	
every day templates, macros, etc.	x	x	x	
monthly/quarterly statements	x	x		
practice evaluation reports	x	x	x	

Team

	Need	Available from Firm	Advisor Paid Created or Modified	External Supplier
team member salaries	x	3	3.5	
team member bonuses	x	0	6.5	
team appreciation events	x	x	x	
gifts to team members	x		x	

Training/Education:Advisor & Team

	Need	Available from Firm	Advisor Paid Created or Modified	External Supplier
software	x	x	x	x
marketing	x	x	x	x
practice management	x	x	x	x
client communication	x	x	x	x
investing	x	x	x	x
financial planning	x	x	x	x
tax	x	x	x	x

Client Education

	Need	Available from Firm	Advisor Paid Created or Modified	External Supplier
mutual fund reports	x	x	x	x
separately managed acct reports	x	x	x	x
market history reports	x	x	x	x
RRSP, RRIF, TFSA, RESP info	x	x		x
life insurance strategy info	x	x	x	x
income replacement info	x	x		x
estate planning strategy info	x	x		x
POA, executor, trustee info	x	x		x
tax strategy reports	x	x		x
government budget reports	x	x		x

Marketing

website builder	x	x	x	
brochures online	x	x	x	
client appreciation events	rare	partial	very rare	
client gifts	x		x	
Andex Charts	x			fund cos

Investment Research

mutual fund analysis	x	x		x
money manager due diligence	x	x	x	x
common stocks (in-house)	rare	x		
preferred shares (in-house)	x	x		
client online access to research	x	x		
Bloomberg	x	x		
external source: _Credit Suisse_	rare	x		
external source: _Value Line_	rare	x		

Specialists

insurance	x	x		
trust and estate planning	x	x		x
legal	x	x		x
tax	x	x		x

Office

real estate: _location, space_	x	x		
advisor private office	x			
home office	x		x	
remote access: _advisor & team_	x	x	x	
computer hardware	x	x		
furnishings	x	x	x	
printers, fax, scanners, etc.	x	partial	partial	
office materials	x	partial	partial	
mail services	x	x		
courier services	x		x	

COMMENTS

I was sure to recognize events in client's lives (death in family, etc.) with
a gift or donation.

C Timms Sample (Advisor Name)
Summary of Pricing & Client Costs
Date

Direct Charges

Commission/Transaction/Trading Charges	Incurred	Frequency
purchase of bond _0.2%/yr, max 1%_	x	at execution
sale of bond _0 - 0.2%/yr, max 1%_	x	at execution
purchase of preferred share _0.2%/yr, max 1%_	x	at execution
sale of preferred share _0.2%/yr, max 1%_	x	at execution
buy common stock _min $140 , max 1% (unsol)_	occasional	at execution
sale common stock _min $140, max 1% (unsol)_	occasional	at execution
mutual fund redemption fees	rare	at execution

Advisor Annual Fee % Based on Client Assets		
cash: _0.0%_	x	quarterly
gov't guaranteed bonds/GICs: _0.2%_	x	quarterly
preferred shares: _0.2% big bank rate reset_	x	quarterly
equity mutual funds: _1.0% F-series_	x	quarterly
separately managed equity: _1.5% - 2.25%_	x	quarterly
minimum annual: _$2,000 ($0 advisor managed)_	x	quarterly

Administration/Operating Charges		
admin fee (RRSP, RRIF, LIF, etc.): _$125_	x	annually
TFSA fee: _$75 ($0:fee-based/assets >$100,000)_	rare	annually
RESP fee: _$75 ($0:fee-based/assets >$100,000)_	rare	annually
small household fee: _($125-$250)_	rare	annually
special account fee: _$200 ($0 if fee-based)_	rare	annually
transfer out fee: _$100_	x	annually
banking fee (wiring, etc.)	x	on execution
safekeeping fees (paper certificates): _____	rare	annually

Indirect Charges	Incurred	Frequency
trailing commissions (mutual funds, ETFs)	x	monthly
fees embedded in financial products (GICs, etc.)	x	on execution
product fees (commission paid by supplier)	rare	on execution
fund management fees	x	
mutual fund MERs: _1.0% - 1.35%_	x	
mutual fund trading fees (TER)	x	

Indirect Charges (continued)

	Incurred	Frequency
new issue commissions paid by issuer	x	on execution
fees embedded in life annuity products	x	on execution
fees embedded in life insurance products	x	on execution
referral fees:_advisor pays for receiving referral_	rare	varies
finders fees:_ advisor paid for finding a mortgage_	rare	on execution

COMMENTS

I gradually changed most clients to fee-based (over 70%).

Some clients have kept a transaction account for their own stock picking.

Segmented Clientele Communication Service Model Sample

To facilitate the articulation of an advisor's approach to segmenting their clientele, I have created separate checklist templates with items identical to those previously described for each service model category, including columns for four client segments. Both the template and a sample are downloadable from my website. The following is the fictitious sample summary for a segmenting advisor's client communication service model.

Segmenting Advisor Sample (Advisor Name)
Summary Of Service Model for Client Communication

	Client Segment			
	A	B	C	D
Client Contact Methods				
personal phone calls with updates	monthly	quarterly	semi-annually	annually
personal phone calls re transactions	as needed	as needed	as needed	as needed
voicemail for incoming calls	after hours only	after hours only	after hours only	after hours only
personal e-mail	as needed	as needed	as needed	as needed
face-to-face review at advisor's office	semi-annually	annually	as needed	on request
face-to-face review at client's location	as needed	on request	on request	on request
online review	as needed	as needed	as needed	on request
mailout/e-mail review	semi-annually	as needed	annually	on request
market update letters/e-mails	mass blast, quarterly	mass blast, quarterly	mass blast, quarterly	mass blast, quarterly
money manager update letters/e-mails	group blast, as needed	group blast, as needed	group blast, as needed	group blast, as needed
stock update letters/e-mails	group blast, as needed	group blast, as needed	group blast, as needed	group blast, as needed
newsletters	mass blast, quarterly	mass blast, quarterly	mass blast, quarterly	mass blast, quarterly
website postings	available to all	available to all	available to all	available to all
blogs	available to all	available to all	available to all	available to all
videos	available to all	available to all	available to all	available to all
podcasts	available to all	available to all	available to all	available to all
Client Reminders				
maturing GICs, CSBs, bonds, etc.	as needed	as needed	as needed	as needed
RRSP contributions	annually	annually	annually	annually
TFSA contributions	annually	annually	annually	annually
RESP contributions	annually	annually	annually	annually
life insurance premium reminders	annually	annually	annually	annually

Client Reminders (continued)

	A Clients	B Clients	C Clients
disability insurance premium reminders	annually	annually	annually
critical illness premium reminders	annually	annually	annually
RRSP conversion to RRIF/annuity	annually	annually	annually
LIRA conversion to LRIF/annuity	annually	annually	annually
tax loss selling	annually	annually	

Personal Touches

	A Clients	B Clients	C Clients
holiday season cards	annually	annually	annually
team picture	annually	annually	annually
family picture	10 clients annually		
holiday season gifts	annually		
sympathy cards/gifts	as needed		
personal celebration gifts	as needed		
birthday cards/letters	annually		
birthday calls	annually		
sports/entertainment tickets	annually		
individual client lunches/dinners	annually	sometimes	
individual client entertainment events	annually		
book gifts	sometimes	sometimes	sometimes
referral thank-you calls	every referral	every referral	every referral
referral thank-you gifts	every referral	sometimes	sometimes

COMMENTS

A Clients: also included some clients with lower production but huge potential.

B Clients: also included some clients with big potential.

The contact management system provides daily team member reminders to provide service to particular clients.

Acknowledgements

My husband, Adrian Bannister, has been wonderfully encouraging and supportive of me in all my endeavours through the last 17 years of my career and the years it has taken me to write these handbooks. He has put up with my moods during stressful periods as an advisor, (the financial crisis comes to mind), as well as the trials and tribulations of my learning the process of writing and publishing these books. He has been a valuable sounding board and served as a test reader, editor and technical advisor. Adrian sometimes remembered important topics, issues and things I did during my career that I neglected to include in my early drafts. I feel very fortunate and thankful for his many contributions to my life and career.

I was extremely fortunate when a former associate of mine, Mike Bishop, agreed to work part-time with me to assist me with these books. He worked on my team for 18 years before I retired from my financial advice practice. Mike served as my editor, tech expert and sometimes as my memory and co-writer. I will be forever grateful for his help.

My practice's clients provided me with many of the ideas discussed in this book through their questions, requests and by sharing their life and business experiences with me. Thank you for all of your support and wonderful conversations throughout my career.

I have been very fortunate to draw upon many friends and contacts in the financial services industry while in the process of writing and publishing these handbooks. Many of these people served as test readers and editors, sometimes helping me to remember topics or issues that I needed to address in the books. Others simply provided much needed encouragement for me to share my experience and knowledge. I have listed the names in alphabetical order: Sonia Baxendale, John-Paul Bernardi, Rob Blagojevic, Laura Cameron, Rose Cammareri, Sandy Cardy, Dianne Carruthers, Susan Carson, Jonathan Carter, James Collins, Cindy Crean, Megan Deeks, Wilma Ditchfield, Dan Downing, Stephen Dunn, Tim Eastwood, Carole Foster, Steve Geist, Monique Gravel, Rollie Guenette, Tony Johnson, Mark Kalichman, Katie Keir, Steven Krupika, Mara Ladico, Christine Lam, Grace Lutfy, Carol Lynde, Rod Mahrt, Paul Maranger, Gaelan Martin–Timms, Gary Mayzes, Jeff McCartney, B.K. Milne, Bruce Moore, Paul Musson, Katie Ophelders, Gabby Pulcini, Kevin Punshon, Jerry Rawlik, Meri Rawling-Taylor, Ann Richards, Tammie Rix, Stephanie Sienko, Mark Slater, Lois Smith, Sean Struthers, Iris Sugiyama, Rory Tufford, Timothy Tufford, Maili Wong.

Thanks to Ryan Levesque for his patience and advice while guiding me through the self publishing process.

Thanks to Melissa Levesque for her patience and help designing the covers and the formatting of the various forms of this handbook.

About the Author

Personal Background

Christine Timms was born into a family of small business owners, the youngest of five children all born within six years. She worked several part-time jobs as a teenager as she grew up in a small town in Southern Ontario, Canada. She put herself through university thanks, in large part, to the co-op work/study program at the University of Waterloo. Christine was always very competitive in sports, school and business, never shying away from a challenge. She is a lifelong fan of the Toronto Raptors, the Toronto Blue Jays, the Buffalo Bills and Canadian tennis players. Christine lives in Toronto, Canada with her husband and son.

Financial Services Career

As Christine began to understand herself more in the early years of her professional career, she realized that she needed to see a direct relationship between her efforts and success. She wanted to be her own boss and build her own business with no glass ceiling. She had always been curious about investing, was interested in teaching and enjoyed working with people. Christine wanted the freedom to think for herself and give independent advice to clients she could work with continuously over the life of her career. Christine had a competitive nature and sought an opportunity to be judged based on quantifiable results, effectively eliminating the glass ceiling. Christine determined the best opportunity to combine these interests and goals was through the career of a full-service investment advisor.

Christine was hired and trained by Merrill Lynch Canada in 1983. She began her career as an advisor with no clients after working for three years as an internal auditor for the Canadian Federal Government. She became an advisor at CIBC Wood Gundy when they bought Merrill Lynch Canada in 1990 and remained with CIBC Wood Gundy until retirement.

- Christine achieved chairman's club in her firm for the first time in 1993 and every year thereafter during her career (24 years in a row) including 2016, her last year as an advisor. Chairman's club included the top performers of the firm (usually approximately the top 8% of the firm's advisors).

- Christine served on CIBC Wood Gundy's Retail Advisory Board (committee of advisors assembled to provide feedback to firm management) from November 1995 to September 1999.

- Christine retired December 1, 2016 after 33 years as an investment advisor with career highs in both assets under management ($400 million) and annual revenue generated. Upon retirement, Christine's clientele consisted of about 350 households, with over a third of those households having over $1,000,000 in assets under management with Christine and her team. The clientele included people from all walks of life and occupations: professionals, small business owners, public service workers, skilled trade workers, retirees, widows, etc. Almost all clients were located in the Greater Toronto Area.

Educational History

1980 Bachelor of Mathematics (B. Math)
1982 Certified Management Accountant (CMA, CPA)
1983 Canadian Securities Course (CSC), options
1993 Chartered Investment Manager (CIM)
1995 Life Insurance and Accident & Sickness Insurance Licence
2000 Professional Financial Planning (PFP)
2010 Registered Retirement Consultant (RRC)
2015 Certified Executor Advisor (CEA)

Christine no longer holds any licence to practice as a financial advisor.

Books by Christine Timms

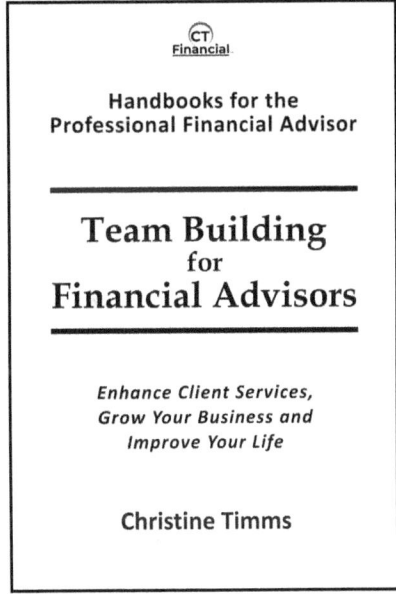

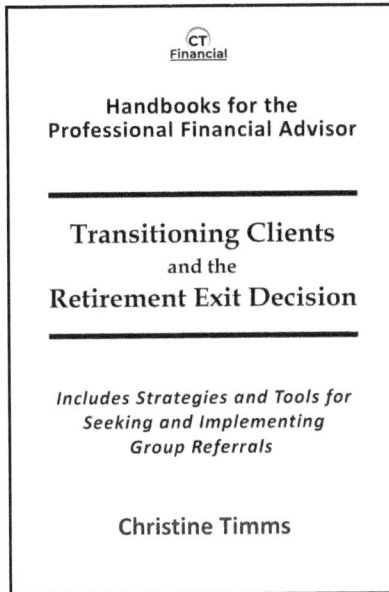

CT
Financial

**Handbooks for the
Professional Financial Advisor**

Business Models
for
Financial Advisors

---

*Develop and Articulate Your
Unique Business Model*

Christine Timms

CT
Financial

**Handbooks for the
Professional Financial Advisor**

Team Building
for
Financial Advisors

---

*Enhance Client Services,
Grow Your Business and
Improve Your Life*

Christine Timms

CT
Financial

**Handbooks for the
Professional Financial Advisor**

Transitioning Clients
and the
Retirement Exit Decision

---

*Includes Strategies and Tools for
Seeking and Implementing
Group Referrals*

Christine Timms

Templates Available on
www.christinetimms.com

Business Models for Financial Advisors

Identify the Most Compatible Clients for Your Practice checklists
- Identify Compatible Groups of Clients and Potential Clients
- Identify Criteria for Sustainable Individual Relationships

Articulate Your Unique Service Model checklists
- Client Communication
- Investing
- Financial Planning
- Tax Strategies and Return Preparation

Determine Needed Resources and Suppliers checklists

Establish Pricing and Client Costs Model checklists

Choose Advisor Compensation Structure and Career Path
 checklists

Segmenting Clientele - Segmentation Criteria worksheet

Segmented Clientele Unique Service Model checklists

Client Investment Allocation Decision Flow Chart (free)

Team Building for Financial Advisors

Team Payroll Sensitivity Analysis spreadsheet

Advisor Actual Team Compensation Costs spreadsheet

Team Member Duty Distribution List - Associate Structure

Team Member Duty Distribution List - Specialist Structure

Transitioning Clients and the Retirement Exit Decision

Business Model Checklists (as shown in Business Models for
 Financial Advisors)

Steps of Transition Timeline checklist (free)

Potential Successor(s) Evaluation worksheet (free)

Sample Retirement Phone Call Script (free)

Sample Formal Retirement Letter (free)

www.ingramcontent.com/pod-product-compliance
Lightning Source LLC
Chambersburg PA
CBHW071422210326
41597CB00020B/3614